THE CRAFT -A-DAY BOOK

30 PROJECTS TO MAKE WITH RECYCLED MATERIALS

For my mom. Thank you for passing along that creative spark. —K.C.

For my crafty mom —J.S.L.

Twenty-First Century Books
A division of Lerner Publishing Group, Inc.
241 First Avenue North
Minneapolis, MN 55401 USA

For reading level and more information, look up this title at www.lernerbooks.com.

Additional images: Kari Cornell pp. 22, 34 (right); 73, 83 (both) 102, 110 (both); Laura Westlund/Independent Picture Service (illustrations); PremiumVector/Shutterstock.com (letters); iStock.com/ksushsh (paper); vvoe/Shutterstock.com (needle); Paladin12/Shutterstock.com (paper); donatas1205/Shutterstock.com (buttons); Lainea/Shutterstock.com (tape); MNI/Shutterstock.com (scissors); DTraves/Shutterstock.com (pins).

Main body text set in Avenir LT Pro 45 Book 11/15.
Typeface provided by Linotype AG.

Library of Congress Cataloging-in-Publication Data

Names: Cornell, Kari A., author. | Larson, Jennifer S., 1967– photographer (expression)
Title: The craft-a-day book : 30 projects to make with recycled materials / by Kari Cornell ; photographs by Jennifer S. Larson.
Description: Minneapolis : Twenty-First Century Books, 2018. | Includes bibliographical references and index. | Audience: Ages 13–18. | Audience: Grades 9 to 12.
Identifiers: LCCN 2017009911 (print) | LCCN 2017029125 (ebook) | ISBN 9781512498813 (eb pdf) | ISBN 9781512413137 (lb : alk. paper)
Subjects: LCSH: Handicraft—Juvenile literature.
Classification: LCC TT160 (ebook) | LCC TT160 .C6765 2018 (print) | DDC 745.5—dc23

LC record available at https://lccn.loc.gov/2017009911

Manufactured in the United States of America
1-39766-21310-8/2/2017

THE CRAFT -A-DAY BOOK

30 PROJECTS TO MAKE WITH RECYCLED MATERIALS

KARI CORNELL

PHOTOGRAPHS BY JENNIFER S. LARSON

TWENTY-FIRST CENTURY BOOKS / MINNEAPOLIS

TABLE OF CONTENTS

INTRODUCTION
FINDING INSPIRATION

If you're reading this, you probably like making things from scratch. Maybe you knit your own hats, sew your own pajama pants, make your own jewelry, love to draw, or do origami. Or perhaps you don't really do any of these things, but you'd like to begin. On the pages of this book, you'll find instructions for thirty projects. You'll also find ideas for discovering your own creative path. Soon you'll be dreaming up projects that are uniquely yours, handstamped with your individual sense of style.

THE CREATIVE PROCESS AT WORK

How do you find the inspiration to create? Inspiration can be found anywhere, from the gingko leaves that you step over on the sidewalk on the way home from the bus stop to the box of cast-off buttons at a secondhand shop. Inspiration also lives on the pages of favorite magazines or online catalogs, in the window displays at your go-to clothing or gift stores, in graffiti murals, or in the set design of the movie you saw the other night. Even the time spent waiting in lines at school, at the fair, or at the mall can turn up inspiring ideas. Study patterns on clothing, color combinations in magazines, store signage and window displays, or the packaging of your favorite products. All of these come from the creative process at work. You can use these ideas as a springboard for your own creativity.

Learning to look closely at the world around you is a fabulous way to find inspiration. While walking to a friend's house, keep an eye out for interesting patterns in nature—the shape of ice crystals and raindrops or the texture and pattern of the bark on a tree. Try including one of these patterns or shapes in your next art or craft project. You don't have to get it perfect to create something beautiful.

HOW HARD CAN IT BE?

This craft book offers a range of activities. Some are super easy, requiring very few tools and supplies; a couple of easy steps such as cutting and pasting; and very little time to complete. Others are intermediate level, requiring more tools and supplies; or more steps, difficult steps, or both (such as multiple foldings or making templates, then sewing, then embroidering); and more time to finish. Advanced projects don't necessarily require lots of tools and supplies and lots of steps, but they will definitely require more time and, in some cases, several techniques to make the finished craft. Start easy and work your way up. What you once thought was a harder craft will soon become easy. Choose what you're in the mood for!

The crafts are ranked as Easy, Intermediate, or Advanced. Look for these icons:

 Easy

Intermediate

Advanced

You don't have to leave the house to find ideas either. The creative spark for your next project—and maybe even the materials you need to create it—might be right under your nose. Ordinary household items that may otherwise be doomed for the thrift store box or the recycling bin may be just what you need. You can work with them to make something fun and whimsical or revive something that's tired but still useful. Bring your own experiences, materials, and tastes to any project to truly make it your own.

CHALLENGE YOURSELF!

If you're feeling stuck and can't come up with any ideas, challenge yourself! Jump-start your creativity by setting a goal to do something creative every day or every other day for a week or even a month. For thirty days, I dreamed up projects using materials I had at home, allowing ideas that came to me during each day to be my guides.

One day, after discovering a shoe box filled with striped socks with holes in the heels, I decided to make something useful out

of them. I dumped the multicolored socks on the floor and began cutting off the feet. After arranging the socks in a row, I studied the order and color combinations. And then I did some rearranging. I pulled out my sewing machine and started sewing the socks together. I had a fun new scarf in just 20 minutes!

On another day, a pile of old sweaters inspired me. I took a plain, light blue crewneck sweater that I hadn't worn for a couple of years and paired it with an old polka-dot pajama top that was way too big for me. I cut the row of buttons and buttonholes off the pajama top. Then I cut open the sweater down the middle of the front panel. This created a cardigan style. To finish off the edges of the front panels, I sewed the button and buttonhole rows from the pajama top to the edge of each sweater panel. I've always preferred cardigans anyway. Best of all, the sweater was unique to me. No one else would have one quite like it, and I could wear it knowing my own creativity infused every stitch.

These two projects (and 28 more) came to be because I pushed myself to create. I set a few rules and went for it. I posted the projects on social media each day to hold myself accountable—and to share my ideas with other people. Give it a try, and see what you can do!

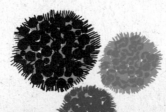

THE RULES

The rules I established were simple, designed to open my mind and promote greater creativity.

Rule 1: Don't worry about finishing the projects in one day. This meant that I had a number of projects to complete by the end of the month. Starting them was all the motivation I needed to get them done later.

Rule 2: Don't limit yourself to one type of project. Creativity can happen with a ball of yarn and needles; cloth and a sewing machine; a saucepan, fresh ingredients, and a stove; or a trowel and seeds in the garden. Let whatever inspires you on a given day guide you.

Rule 3: Whenever possible, use materials and supplies that you already have on hand. I didn't want to spend time shopping for materials, especially since I had a healthy stash of sweaters, cast-off fabrics, and striped socks without mates. It's so satisfying to make something clever out of items that seemed destined for the trash or thrift store bag. Not only are you reusing and keeping things out of landfills, but you're not buying more unneeded stuff.

HUNTING FOR MATERIALS

Looking for the materials for a project is an exciting part of making any craft. Learn to scavenge. For example, it's fun to make projects with items you already have. I always have a box of fabric scraps, a bag of reusable ribbons, a tin of old buttons, a box of gift bags from last year's presents, and a stash of yarn left over from knitting projects. For many of the projects in this book, you can find materials and inspiration by sorting through your recycling bins. If you don't have all of these materials at home, look for them at school or at your after-school job. It's easy to find free or low-cost materials. Here are some ideas to get started:

Materials swap. One way to gather free supplies (and get rid of items you're not using) is to host a materials swap. Think of three or four friends who like to craft and may have additional supplies. Pick a date, time, and place to meet. Then gather all of your old sweaters, button-up shirts, buttons, and other scrap items that you don't mind parting with and invite your friends to trade materials. This is a great way to add "new" items to your craft stash without spending a dime!

And don't forget to ask your neighbors and relatives too. Your grandparents, for example, might have cool stuff to work with. Or maybe one of your neighbors is into craft projects too. They may have good crafting materials to swap or to give to you.

Secondhand stores. Shops such as Goodwill, Salvation Army, or independent thrift shops are great places to look for colorful sweaters, lampshades, yarn, T-shirts with eye-catching patterns, or anything else to complete your project. Think of items that might work as unique embellishments as well, like vintage jewelry, scarves, ribbons, buttons, or decorative flowers. Most items at these types of stores are not expensive.

Garage sales. Also known as yard sales, thrift sales, and tag sales, these sidewalk sales are a great place to find used clothing, crafting supplies, or household goods at very low prices. You also may be able to find sewing supplies or a stash of old buttons. Invite a friend to go with you.

At secondhand stores and garage sales, inspect any clothing or other items you want to buy for holes, stains, missing pieces such as buttons or zippers, and other signs of wear. Some holes or stains may be OK, especially if they are in an area that you won't see or be using anyway. Buttons can be easy to replace. Zippers are a little trickier.

Craft supply store. Your local craft store or paper and stationery supply store is a good place to find extra buttons, thread, fabric, ribbons, yarn, paper, or any other supplies for your project. Look for sale bins in these stores, especially after holidays. You can often find supplies for 50 percent off or more.

Dollar store. Don't forget to look for supplies at your local dollar or discount store. These shops tend to be a good place to find party supplies and decorations that could lend a touch of color or pattern to paper-based projects.

Online supplies. Be sure to check online sources for cheap craft supplies. Check www.createforless.com for the Free Stuff Friday giveaway deals.

MAKING IT YOUR OWN

What is it about your favorite things that make them truly your own? Think of the T-shirt you love the most. It's probably your favorite because it's appealing in lots of different ways. It may be a color you love. It may have a photo of your favorite band or characters from a video game you're wild about. Besides how it looks, the shirt might fit you really well or be made of supersoft cotton that feels cozy against your skin. These "best things ever" make your T-shirt something you want to wear every day.

When you start a project, think about how to add that personal "best ever" touch. Think about what colors make you happy. Do you want to go with patterned or plain, simple or fancy, modern or vintage? All of these decisions come into play when you think about embellishing your project—or not. The final product will be a unique expression of your tastes and your personality.

TOOLS TO HAVE ON HAND

There are a few go-to tools for many of the projects in this book. Here's a quick rundown of what you'll need:

Craft knife. This cutting tool is shaped like a pen and has a sharp razor blade attached to the end. It's great for making precise cuts in the hand-cut snowflakes and favorite paper votive projects.

Drill with bits. An electric or battery-powered drill with a set of bits is helpful although not necessary for creating holes in the hand-cut snowflakes project.

Fabric marking pen, chalk, pen, or pencil. Any of these marking tools will work. A writing tool is for creating pattern templates on paper and for marking spots for placement on fabrics.

Iron and ironing board. An iron and ironing board are useful for applying fusible interfacing to T-shirts and removing wrinkles from fabrics and tagboard.

Iron-on tear-away stabilizer. Iron-on stabilizer, available at craft and fabric stores, adds a stiff back layer to knit fabrics, making them easier to sew or embroider. For the projects in this book, use white stabilizer.

Mod Podge. This versatile glue and protective coating for paper projects is available at craft stores and big-box stores. It comes in matte and gloss finishes. Gloss dries to a shiny, bright finish. Matte dries to a flat, or less shiny, finish. You can use either one, depending on the look you want for the finished craft. You can also find recipes online for making your own Mod Podge-style glue. It's an easy and affordable alternative.

Newspaper. The lightweight pages from a newspaper are useful for creating pattern templates and for protecting surfaces while you work.

Paintbrush. Use a 1-inch (2.5 cm) trim painting brush to apply Mod Podge to projects.

Paper punch. Available at craft stores, paper supply stores, and big-box stores, this handy tool looks a bit like a stapler and punches circles from sheets of paper. The projects in this book call for a ½-inch (1.3 cm) punch and a 2½-inch (6.4 cm) punch.

Pom-pom maker. This round plastic tool is available at craft stores or online and is used to make yarn pom-poms. Instructions for how to make your own pom-pom maker from cardboard are included in this book.

Scissors. Use a sharp pair of scissors for cutting out papers, pattern templates, and fabrics. Ideally, keep one scissors for paper and another for fabrics.

Sewing machine. Libraries and community centers often have sewing machines that patrons can use. Or you may be able to borrow one, or buy one used at a thrift shop or yard sale. If you don't have a manual, look for one online for your make and model.

Straight pins. Straight steel-head sewing pins are useful for attaching paper patterns to fabric and for attaching parts of a sewing project together.

Tape measure or ruler. Either of these tools can be used to measure pattern pieces on paper or fabric.

SAFETY TIPS

Crafting involves a wide range of tools, supplies, materials, products, and techniques. Here are some commonsense tips for staying safe while you work on your projects. Whenever you're in doubt, ask an adult or an experienced crafter for help. You will see these safety icons in the book:

Candles. When using candles, remember to never leave them unattended. They are a fire hazard. If you are moving to a different room or leaving the house, blow out the candles before you go. Battery-operated tea lights, available at hardware stores or many big-box stores, are a safe alternative to real candles.

Hammer and nails. For the crafts in this book, you can use a small hammer. Be sure to grip the handle firmly, and keep your eyes on the nails you are pounding so you don't hammer your fingers by mistake. And be sure to use clean nails or new nails. Rusty nails can lead to infection.

Craft knives. When using a craft knife, always keep your hands out of the path of the blade. If you have difficulty cutting through layers of paper, trace over the line several times with the blade, applying a consistent amount of pressure with control. Avoid applying too much pressure. Cover the blade whenever it's not in use.

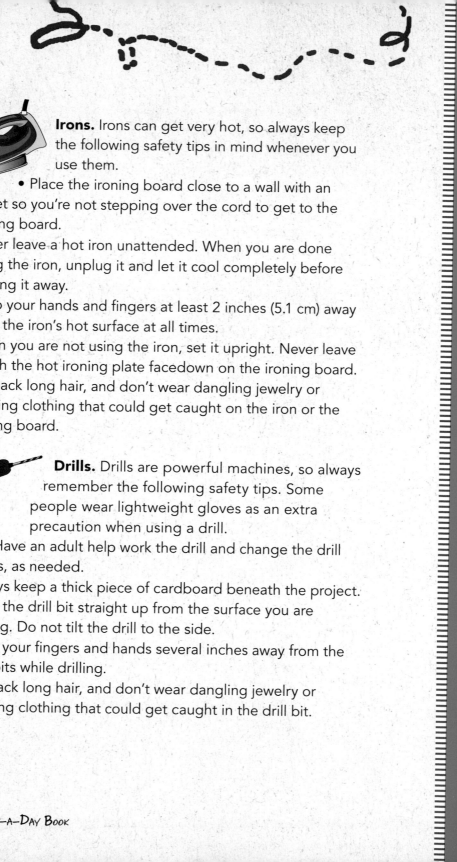

Irons. Irons can get very hot, so always keep the following safety tips in mind whenever you use them.

- Place the ironing board close to a wall with an outlet so you're not stepping over the cord to get to the ironing board.
- Never leave a hot iron unattended. When you are done using the iron, unplug it and let it cool completely before putting it away.
- Keep your hands and fingers at least 2 inches (5.1 cm) away from the iron's hot surface at all times.
- When you are not using the iron, set it upright. Never leave it with the hot ironing plate facedown on the ironing board.
- Tie back long hair, and don't wear dangling jewelry or draping clothing that could get caught on the iron or the ironing board.

Drills. Drills are powerful machines, so always remember the following safety tips. Some people wear lightweight gloves as an extra precaution when using a drill.

- Have an adult help work the drill and change the drill bits, as needed.
- Always keep a thick piece of cardboard beneath the project.
- Align the drill bit straight up from the surface you are drilling. Do not tilt the drill to the side.
- Keep your fingers and hands several inches away from the drill bits while drilling.
- Tie back long hair, and don't wear dangling jewelry or draping clothing that could get caught in the drill bit.

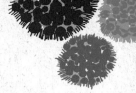

 **Sewing machines.** Sewing machines can be powerful machines, especially when they are stitching rapidly. Some commonsense safety tips include these:

- Ask an adult to help you if you are not completely confident in your sewing skills.
- It's OK to be on the safe side and sew slowly. As you gain confidence with your skills and the fabrics you are working with, you can sew more rapidly though always at a moderate speed.
- Always keep your fingers out of the way of the needle when it is moving, no matter how slowly.
- Keep the work space where you are sewing free of everything but the fabric, scissors, pin cushion, and instructions you are working with. To avoid spills and other accidents, keep your can of pop (or other liquids), tools, and supplies nearby, but not on the same surface as the sewing machine.

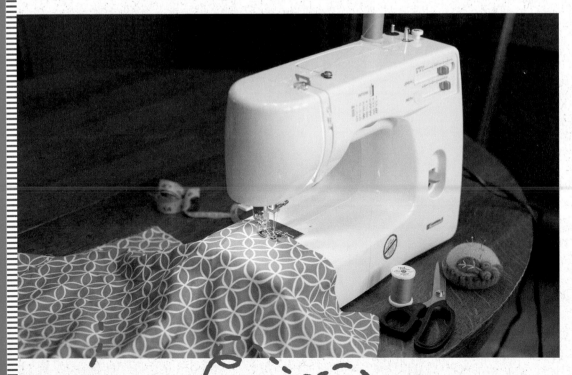

CHAPTER 1

LIGHT UP THE NIGHT

I've always been entranced and calmed by the warm glow of candlelight and mood-setting lamps. I love the way patterns of shadow and light are reflected around the room. The light brightens the darkest nights of winter and is such a perfect alternative to overhead lighting. I also like to strategically place candles or mood-setting lamps in dim corners of the house. You'll find a mix of mood lighting and candle projects in this chapter, all of them guaranteed to add a gentle glow and cheer to a room.

TIN CAN LUMINARY

I love this project. The hammered holes scatter the light in cool patterns around the room. It is especially fun around Halloween. You can take your hammer and nails to a pumpkin too, creating a similar effect.

INSPIRATION

A friend of mine had a gorgeous luminary made from an old tin can. It was brushed and tarnished and barely recognizable as a tin can. The craftsman who made it was a blacksmith. He used very hot temperatures to cut and shape the can, making it bow out in the middle for a unique look. I loved it and wanted one for myself. This project is an easy riff on the original that inspired it, mainly because I'm no blacksmith. It's fun to make the luminary in different sizes. If you have a part-time job at a restaurant or if your parents belong to a food warehouse club, see if you can find one of the really huge tin cans that beans or coffee come in. Your friends will be really jealous of your giant tin can luminary!

TIN CAN LUMINARY HOW-TO

You Will Need
1 to 3 tin cans in assorted sizes, with rough lid edges removed
paper for sketching out and planning your design

Tools
freezer
pencil
cotton cloth to hold the can in place
handful of 3-inch (7.6 cm) nails in different widths
hammer
1 tea light candle

MAKING THE LUMINARY

1. Soak cans in warm, soapy water to remove labels and glue.

2. Fill cans with water, stopping 1 inch (2.5 cm) short of the top.

3. Place cans on a flat surface in the freezer. Freeze until solid. This will ensure that the tin can doesn't buckle as you hammer it.

4. While the cans freeze, plan your design. On paper, draw your design using dots to indicate holes.

5. Remove the first can from the freezer, and set it on its side on the cloth.

6. Align the tip of one of the nails firmly against the outside of the can. Hammer on the nail until it pierces the side of the can. Then remove the nail.

7. Repeat step 6, alternating nail sizes and working your way around the can to pepper the surface with holes. Refer to your design, as needed.

8. When you are happy with how the luminary looks, dump the melting ice from the can into the sink.

9. Carefully dry the inside and outside of the can with the cotton cloth. Do this gently since the inside of the can will be full of sharp edges from the nailing. Place a tea light at the bottom of the can. Repeat the steps with the other tin cans.

PIN-PUNCHED LAMPSHADE

This is such a simple way to add interest to a boring old lampshade. Look for small lamps, small shades, or both at secondhand shops. I found this base and the shade at nearby shops for only two dollars apiece! You might even have a lampshade at home that will work.

INSPIRATION

I was reading a book called *Fearless Drawing: Illustrated Adventures for Overcoming Artistic Adversity* by Kerry Lemon when I came across the idea of creating an image by using a series of pinholes on a piece of paper. Allowing light to play a part in the illustration adds a whole new dimension. What better place to try this technique than on a plain lampshade? I thought. I already had a pale yellow tabletop lamp that I'd found at my favorite local resale shop. One trip to Goodwill to scour their lampshade collection, and I was ready to get started. In the sample lamp, I decided on a simple design along the edges of the shade.

PIN-PUNCHED LAMPSHADE HOW-TO

You Will Need
sketch pad or any other plain sheets of paper
1 plain, paper-based lampshade
1 lamp base
1 lightbulb (check the lamp for the wattage you will need)

Tools
pencil
1 T-pin or large safety pin or needle
clear removable, one-sided tape

DREAM UP A DESIGN

1. Doodle some ideas for your lampshade design on a piece of paper. Simple circles or other basic geometric patterns are easy to start with. Look online for ideas too.

2. Another option is to wrap a sheet of paper around the outside of the shade to trace its contours with a pencil. Then draw your design within those lines.

3. Remember to keep it simple. Too many holes punched too closely together on the shade may cause it to tear or collapse. (Trust me, I know.) The holes on the sample shade worked well at ½-inch (1.3 cm) intervals.

4. After you have sketched your design, start making the pinholes.

PUNCHING OUT THE DESIGN

1. Remove the shade from the lamp base.

2. For a very simple design, eyeballing usually works fine for punching the design. Insert and remove the T-pin, safety pin, or needle into the lampshade at regular intervals to make the design. No need to first copy it onto the shade.

3. For more detailed designs, tape the paper on which you sketched your design to the top edge of the shade. Use removable tape. At regular intervals, carefully punch the T-pin, safety pin, or needle along the lines of your drawing and through the shade.

4. When you have punched out the entire design, remove the paper and tape (if you attached it) and secure the shade to the lamp. Make sure you've put in a lightbulb too. Turn on the lamp to take a look at your work. Fine-tune any details.

CRAFT PAPER LANTERN

This lantern is simple to make and so pretty, especially as a complement to fall colors. I used prepunched packing paper for the lantern, but it's easy enough to make your own punched paper.

INSPIRATION

Sometimes inspiration for a project can come from the most unexpected places. One October day, I had picked up my box of weekly vegetables from the community supported agriculture (CSA) drop-off in my neighborhood. As I unpacked the box, there, beneath the squash, onions, potatoes, and pumpkins, I discovered the fodder for my next project: heavy brown packing paper, prepunched with holes for ventilation.

I immediately knew I wanted to do something crafty with the paper. What shape would it take? Since it was autumn, when darkness falls earlier each evening, I decided I would use this paper for some sort of luminary. I took a tall, luminary vase that I had stashed away in a downstairs closet, wrapped the paper around it, and placed a tea light inside. Perfect!

CRAFT PAPER LANTERN HOW-TO

You Will Need

1 glass luminary vase or drinking glass (I used a 3-inch-diameter, 7.6
   cm, vase, though you can use any size you like)
brown craft paper, brown bag, or other brown paper to cover the
   vase or glass
clear tape or gift wrap tape
1 tea light candle

Tools

tape measure
ruler
pencil
scissors
½-inch (1.3 cm) paper punch, round, flower-shaped, or both

MAKING THE LANTERN

1. Measure the size of the glass luminary vase or drinking glass
    from top to bottom, and write down your height measurement.
    Then wrap the tape measure around the outside of the vase or
    glass to measure around it and add ½ inch (1.3 cm). Write down
    the number. This is your circumference. The height times the
    circumference will be the dimensions of your final piece of craft
    paper. (The sample is 6 inches, or 15.2 cm, tall by 11 inches, or
    28 cm, around.)

2. Use a ruler and pencil to measure and mark the dimensions onto
    the paper. Make sure your sides are square (the corners meet at
    a neat angle and are not crooked). Cut out the rectangle.

3. Place the piece of craft paper on the table in front of you
    so that the long sides are on the top and bottom. Working
    from the bottom to the top, fold up the paper by a width of
    2 inches (5.1 cm).

4. Make an accordion-style strip by lifting the folded, creased edge up and tucking it under the paper, creating another fold that is 2 inches (5.1 cm) above the first fold. Repeat as needed until the entire piece of craft paper is folded into a 2-inch-wide accordion-style strip.

5. Working from one side of the strip to the other, use the paper punch to make holes at regular intervals in the paper strip. Make sure to punch through all the folds of the strip.

6. Unfold the paper, and smooth it out on a tabletop. Wrap the paper tightly around the sides of the votive to flatten out the folds. Secure the two ends of the paper together with small pieces of clear or gift wrap tape. Don't cover any holes.

7. Insert a tea light candle and enjoy!

TISSUE PAPER JAR LUMINARIES

These luminaries cast a cheerful, multicolored glow and are sure to brighten up any room. The best part? These beauties have a mod, sophisticated look yet are super easy to make. And they are a great way to use recycled glass jars and cast-off colored tissue paper. Ready? Let's do it.

INSPIRATION

Recently, my mom gave me a box filled with treasures from my grade school days. In that box, I found a glass jar that I'd covered with a collage of ripped up pieces of tissue paper. I made it in kindergarten and gave it to my mom for Mother's Day. For years, she used it to hold pens and pencils near the computer in the kitchen. As I turned the jar in my hands, I wondered what it would look like illuminated by a candle. Aha! The idea for this project was born. After scouring the recycling tubs for jars and sorting through my box of wrinkled, already-used tissue paper, I got to work.

TISSUE PAPER JAR LUMINARIES HOW-TO

You Will Need

1 recycled food jar, or jars to make several, preferably with a
wide-lid opening
3 or more sheets of tissue paper in different colors (used is fine)
1 small container of Mod Podge
1 tea light candle

Tools

plastic bucket for soaking
scrub brush
newspaper to cover work space
scissors
1 small paintbrush for applying Mod Podge

MAKING THE LUMINARIES

1. If the jar has a paper label, soak it in water for 10 minutes in a
   plastic bucket or in a sink. Then remove the label with a scrub
   brush or your fingernail. Dry the jar well.

2. Cover your work space with a few sheets of newspaper.

3. Over the newspaper, spread out one of the sheets of tissue
   paper. Use your hands to flatten and smooth any wrinkles.

4. Cut squares, rectangles, triangles, circles, or any other shapes
   you want from the tissue paper. They don't have to be perfect.

5. Repeat steps 3 and 4 with all the sheets of tissue paper, until
   you have enough shapes in a variety of colors to make a cool
   pattern on the jar.

6. Apply an even layer of Mod Podge with a small paintbrush to
   one part of the jar.

7. Select a few of the precut shapes in different colors and carefully place them over the glue, using your fingertip to smooth out any wrinkles. Overlap shapes as much or as little as you like, creating a collage of color over the glued area.

8. Repeat steps 6 and 7 until the jar is covered with tissue paper shapes and no glass shows through. Set the jar aside to dry overnight.

9. The next day, use the paintbrush to apply a layer of Mod Podge over the tissue paper shapes. Be careful when brushing over edges of the tissue paper shapes. If they are not fully adhered to the jar, a swipe of the brush can pull the tissue off. Allow the jars to dry. Drop a tea light (real or battery-operated) in the jar, and light it up!

FAVORITE PAPER VOTIVE

With a little Mod Podge, a strip of pretty patterned paper, and a glass vase (square is my favorite, but a round jar with nontapered sides will work), you can do this craft in no time. And it makes a fantastic gift—if you can stand to part with it.

INSPIRATION

I love the patterned paper I used for this project. I originally bought it to cover the leaves of a bedside table. But when I unearthed a square luminary vase from a cabinet while cleaning, I knew I had to use the paper to make a votive. The flowers look like dahlias to me. The creamy outlines of the flower petals capture the candlelight while the translucent red background glows beautifully. Look for these same qualities in the paper you select for this project. As you are choosing your paper, hold different papers up to a light to see which one glows the most. That's the paper to go with!

FAVORITE PAPER VOTIVE HOW-TO

You Will Need

1 square glass luminary vase
1 sheet of patterned paper, large enough to fit the circumference
    of the vase
1 small container of Mod Podge
1 tea light candle

Tools

tape measure
pencil
yardstick or ruler
scissors
1 small paintbrush for applying glue
craft knife

MAKING THE VOTIVE

1. Use a tape measure to measure the circumference of the vase
    (around all sides). Write down the measurement.

2. Lay the paper on the worktable and place one side of the
    vase on top of the paper. Move the top edge of the vase so
    it aligns along the top corner of the paper. Mark a straight
    line on the paper along the bottom of the vase. Set the vase
    aside. Continue the straight line on the patterned paper, using
    a yardstick or ruler to mark the measurement you recorded in
    step 1.

3. Cut along the line you've just drawn. To test the fit, wrap the
    cut strip of paper around the vase to cover all sides. (Mine was
    a little short, so I cut an extra strip to cover the final corner. Or
    you can start over with another piece of paper.)

4. With the paintbrush, apply an even layer of Mod Podge to one
    side of the vase.

5. Starting from a top corner of the vase, align the top and bottom edges of the patterned paper to the top and bottom of the glued side of the vase. Carefully press the paper against the Mod Podge, smoothing out any wrinkles with your fingers.

6. Turn the vase and apply Mod Podge to the next side, then the paper, working your way around the vase.

7. Once the sides of the vase are completely covered in paper, use a craft knife to trim any excess paper from the top edge. Apply another layer of Mod Podge to the papered surface, and allow to dry overnight. Add a tea light. If you like it, round up more supplies and start the next one!

ORIGAMI PAPER LANTERNS

Once you get the hang of making origami lanterns, it's hard to stop. You'll find yourself making just one more. These cuties also make great gifts. Buy a string of white lights, pull out your collection of origami or wrapping paper, sit down in front of your favorite movie or with a group of friends, and start folding. You'll be done in no time.

INSPIRATION

I first saw these paper lanterns while paging through a magazine during the holiday season. The tiny lanterns were all white, and the string of lights they adorned were hung on a Christmas tree. I loved how the paper boxes captured the glow of the lights. I immediately wanted to fold my own but with patterned papers. I used what I had on hand—a lot of reusable holiday wrapping paper. I strung them all around the living room and dining room. They added such cheer to the rooms! For these paper lights, you can use origami paper, leftover wrapping paper, or any other paper of similar weight. Try making them from the pages of an old novel or from the colorful pages of a secondhand picture book. Tissue paper isn't a good choice. It's too lightweight and tears easily.

● ORIGAMI PAPER LANTERNS HOW-TO

You Will Need
25 pieces of origami paper or another paper of similar weight and of any design and colors you like to make 25 lanterns
1 string of 25 small, white holiday lights

Tools
ruler
pencil

FOLDING THE BOXES

1. Fold the square of paper in half diagonally. Match corners and edges neatly and evenly. Press the ruler gently across the fold to create a crease. Unfold the square. (See origami diagram on pp. 40–41 to follow along.)

2. Fold the same square on the opposite diagonal, following step 1. Unfold.

3. Then fold the paper a third time, this time in half from top to bottom to form a rectangle. Use the ruler to set the crease. Unfold so the wrong side is faceup.

4. Fold in half again, this time from right to left, to make a rectangle the other way. Set the crease with your ruler. Unfold.

CONFUSED?
Origami is fun and easy, once you get the hang of it.
Sometimes it's helpful to use written directions along with a
visual how-to. Check out this easy Wiki tutorial to see how
the origami paper lantern comes together through folding:
http://www.wikihow.com/Make-an-Origami-Balloon.

5. Set the square of paper in front of you wrong side up, and look at the fold lines you just created. You should see eight triangles. Number the triangles with a pencil on the wrong side. Right side up, use the creases you have already made to fold the paper inward so that triangles 1 and 2 are touching each other and triangles 5 and 6 are touching each other. This will create one large triangle with triangles 7 and 8 on top and triangles 3 and 4 on the bottom. Set the triangle in front of you right side up so that the longest side is at the bottom, facing you.

6. Lift the top layer of the bottom-right corner, and fold the corner up to meet the point at the top of the triangle. Crease along the fold you just created.

7. Repeat step 6 with the bottom-left corner. Crease.

8. Flip the triangle over, and repeat steps 6 and 7 with the bottom-right and bottom-left corners on the back layer, creasing each fold. You then have a smaller triangle.

9. Fold the side point (center right) of the top layer to meet the center fold. Then fold the side point (center left) of the top layer to meet the center fold. Crease both folds.

10. Flip your triangle over, and repeat step 9 on the back layer with the center-right and center-left side points. With this folding, you have created four little side pockets, two on the front layer and two on the bottom layer.

11. Use your index finger or pinkie to gently open up the two pockets on the front layer. Then tuck the loose flaps at the top points of your paper into the pockets you just made, tucking the right flap into the right pocket and the left flap into the left pocket. Crease. You don't need to force the entire flap into its pocket, just as much as will easily fit.

12. Flip over and repeat step 11 on the back layer.

13. Find the small hole that you will have created at one tip by folding. Blow gently into the hole to inflate the box. If it doesn't inflate completely, rotate the box a little and blow again gently. If necessary, carefully press or pull on the edges or folds that stick to create smooth surfaces on all sides.

14. Repeat steps 1 through 13 to make the rest of the balloon lanterns.

ATTACHING THE BOXES

1. Gently slip the paper lantern hole over a light on your string of lights.

2. Repeat until you have attached all the lanterns to your string of lights. Hang it over a window, doorway, or archway—or any spot near a plug.

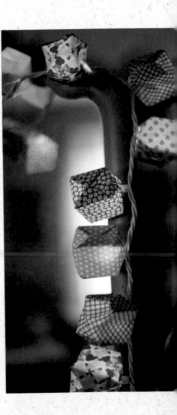

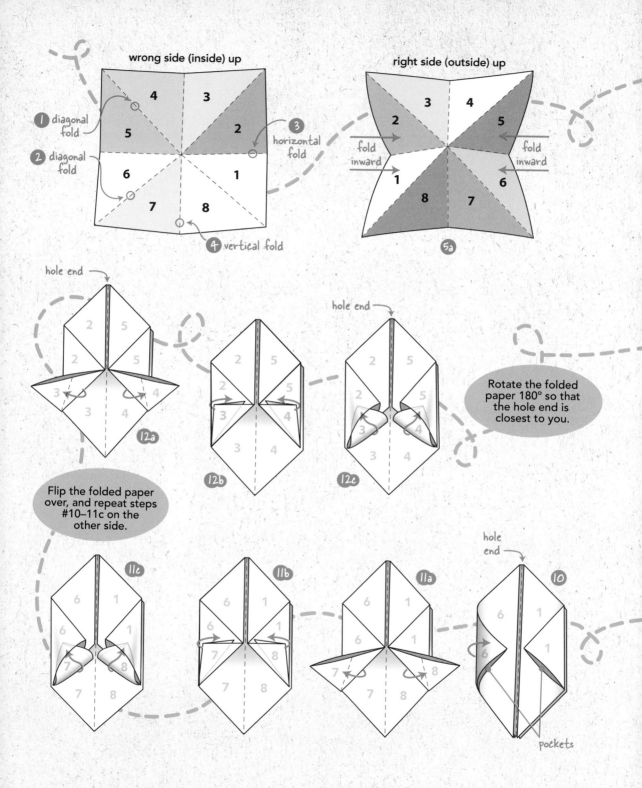

wrong side (inside) up

1 diagonal fold
2 diagonal fold
3 horizontal fold
4 vertical fold

4 3
5 2
6 1
7 8

right side (outside) up

3 4
2 5
fold inward fold inward
1 6
8 7

5a

hole end

2 5
2 5
3 1 4
3 4

12a

2 5
2 5
3 4
3 4

12b

2 5
2 5
3 4
3 4

12c

Rotate the folded paper 180° so that the hole end is closest to you.

Flip the folded paper over, and repeat steps #10–11c on the other side.

hole end

6 1
6 1
7 8
7 8

11c

6 1
6 1
7 8
7 8

11b

6 1
6 1
7 8
7 8

11a

hole end

6 1
6 1

10

pockets

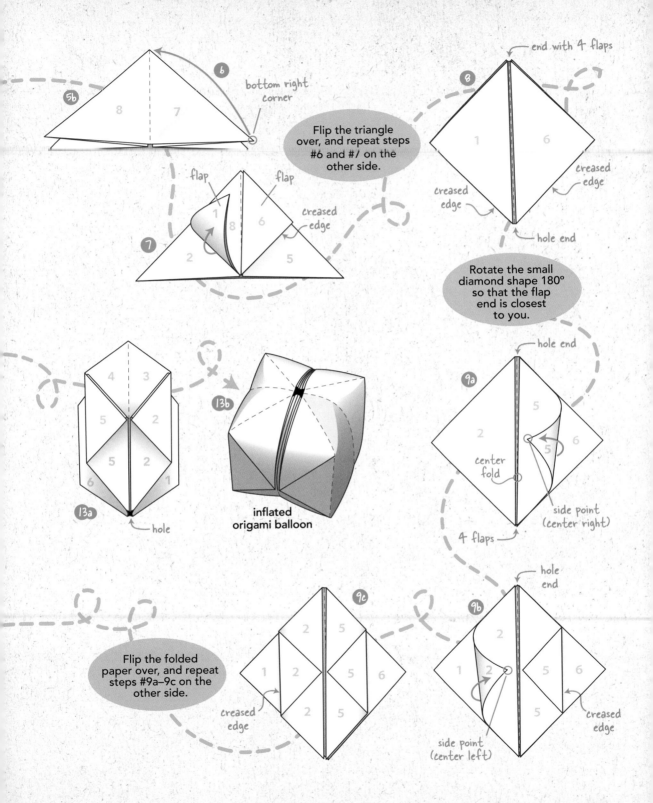

5b

6

bottom right corner

8   7

end with 4 flaps

8

1   6

creased edge

creased edge

hole end

Flip the triangle over, and repeat steps #6 and #7 on the other side.

flap   flap

1   8   6

creased edge

7   2   5

Rotate the small diamond shape 180° so that the flap end is closest to you.

hole end

9a

5

2   5   6

center fold

side point (center right)

4   3

13b

5   2

5   2

6   1

13a

hole

4 flaps

hole end

inflated origami balloon

9c   2   5

1   2   5   6

2   5

creased edge

Flip the folded paper over, and repeat steps #9a–9c on the other side.

9b   2

1   2   5   6

5

creased edge

side point (center left)

CHAPTER 2
PAPER CAPER

I've long had a thing for handmade paper. I love the rough feel of the fibers and the adornments—the flower petals or milkweed tuft, bits of colored paper, or even scraps from the pages of a book—in the mash (paper fiber). I also love patterned paper. For me, these patterns are a way to add color and whimsy to an otherwise ordinary surface.

The projects in this chapter dabble in a wide range of paper crafts, from paper cutting, to printing, and decoupage. You can mix and match the crafts too. Use the hand-printed paper to make origami lanterns or a paper flower garland. If you like to draw, add some of your own illustrations to the cover of your personalized journal or your decoupage tabletop. Experiment and have fun!

HAND-PRINTED WRAPPING PAPER

When you get a package in the mail, you usually keep what's inside the box and throw out the rest. But why not use the packing paper to make your own wrapping paper? It's a quick way to add a handmade touch to gifts—and to rescue packing paper.

INSPIRATION

For this project, I was inspired by a scattering of bright yellow fan-shaped leaves on the sidewalk as I was walking home one autumn day. I knew they were from a gingko tree. I've always loved the shape of gingko leaves. I like that they seem to be aerodynamically designed by Mother Nature to perfectly flutter and drift on the breeze. So I gathered some of the leaves in different sizes and took them home. I was eager to try to replicate their shape on paper. I painted onto the textured side of the leaves and pressed them onto brown packing paper. For variety, I used a leaf rubber stamp and a gold ink stamp pad to add leaves of different shapes to the paper. The green-and-gold leaves made a pretty reminder of my walk home that day. See what you can collect in your neighborhood to make your own printed paper. Maple, elm, and oak leaves work well, especially if they haven't dried out.

HAND-PRINTED WRAPPING PAPER HOW-TO

You Will Need
white or brown packing paper, freezer paper, butcher paper, or tissue wrapping paper

printmaking items such as toilet paper rolls, sheets of plastic packing material, stencils, rubber stamps, just-fallen leaves, fern leaves, tips of evergreen boughs, flower petals, feathers, shells, or rocks

finger paints or inks in different colors

paper towel

Tools
oilcloth, plastic tablecloth, or newspaper

1 small watercolor paintbrush

several plastic lids for mixing paint colors

EXPERIMENT WITH PRINTING MATERIALS

1. Cover your work space with oilcloth, a tablecloth, or newspaper.

2. Spread out a scrap piece of paper, squirt a bit of finger paint or ink into a lid, and take your materials for a test run. You might be surprised by the results. Some items with a lot of texture can be too rigid to work well for printing. They may not bend easily when you press them into the paper, so you won't get the full shape you're looking for. Experiment with a variety of materials to see what works best.

3. For sturdy leaves such as gingko or oak leaves, use the paintbrush to apply the finger paint or ink to the entire surface of the leaf (the most textured side) before pressing the leaf against the paper. For more delicate fern leaves or flower petals, or stencils, set it directly on the paper and use the paintbrush to apply paint or ink over it.

4. As you test the items, keep only the printing materials that work well.

PRINTING

1. On the protected work space, spread a sheet of paper. Smooth out some of the wrinkles with your hands. (The paper doesn't have to be perfectly smooth. Some wrinkling gives the paper character.)

2. Apply paint or ink to your favorite printing item. Press it firmly against the sheet of packing paper, applying it in different areas across the paper. As you go along, you may want to reapply the paint or ink again to make sure the color stays vibrant.

3. On a second piece of paper, combine a variety of printing items using different colors and printing them on the same sheet. Or use the same printing item in several colors on one sheet.

For example, you can use the end of a toilet paper roll dipped in a rainbow of colors. Use a paper towel to wipe off the end before using a new color.

4. When you're done, set the sheets in an out-of-the-way area to dry. Store dry sheets flat in a drawer. You can also roll them up, put a rubber band around the roll, and store them upright in a bin or on a shelf.

DECOUPAGED BEDSIDE TABLE

I rescued this old table from the curb on garbage day one week. With a little creative spark, I transformed it into a bright bedside table. This piece would also make a great coffee table in a small bedroom, apartment, or dorm room. And it's easy to do!

INSPIRATION

I'm obsessed with pretty paper, so I have a lot of it at home. One day, I said to myself, why not use these papers to add a pattern to the surface of my rescued table? It would brighten the table and just about any room. Originally, I had planned to use the patterned paper to cover the table and both of its leaves. But after I'd covered the top, I really liked how the pattern contrasted against the turquoise blue of the table's leaves. So I decided to stop right there. Don't be afraid to change your mind as you work on a project. Sometimes simple is better.

● DECOUPAGED BEDSIDE TABLE HOW-TO

You Will Need

Mod Podge, matte finish

1 small wooden square or rectangular table

1 sheet of decorative paper large enough to cover the table surface
and wrap around the edges

1-quart (1 L) can of fast-drying water-based polyurethane,
matte sheen

Tools ✎

2 paintbrushes (1 for Mod Podge and 1 for polyurethane)

craft knife

COVERING THE TABLE

1. With a paintbrush, apply a thin, even layer of Mod Podge to the
   tabletop and edges. Add a 1-inch (2.5 cm) swipe of Mod Podge
   to the underside of the table, along the edge.

2. Carefully align the paper on the top of the table. Make sure that
   the pattern is straight and that there's an extra couple of inches
   hanging over each of the four edges of the table. Press the
   paper into place.

3. Carefully smooth out any wrinkles along the table surface.

4. Working one edge at a time, wrap the paper around and
   under the table edges. At the corners, wrap the paper
   straight over the edge on one side. Then create a diagonal
   fold with the other edge to cover it, like the crease you
   would make when folding wrapping paper around a
   square box.

5. Check all edges for wrinkles, smoothing any you find.

6. Trim any excess paper with a craft knife. Allow to dry overnight.

7. The next day, brush a layer of Mod Podge onto the entire piece of paper—top, edges, and underneath. Allow it to dry overnight.

8. Use a paintbrush to apply a layer of polyurethane. This protects the paper from water stains and tears. Allow to dry overnight.

PAPER FLOWER GARLAND

This cascading garland is another perfect way to show off a collection of your favorite patterned papers. Make several to create a curtain of blooms in a doorway, window, or on a wall. Make one for your locker at school! Hang vertically for best results.

INSPIRATION

I love the idea of stringing dandelions together to create a chain. But I can count on one hand the number of times I've actually done it. Maybe that's why making this paper garland is so appealing—I finally have a chance to make my own chain of flowers. I'm not sitting in a field of yellow, watching the clouds drift by overhead, but there's definitely something meditative and mindful about the repetitive motions of making this garland. As I cut out the flowers, curl the petals, and string them on a length of ribbon, my mind focuses on the task, forgetting about day-to-day worries. And I love the result—a cascading ribbon of blooms.

PAPER FLOWER GARLAND HOW-TO

You Will Need

1 small piece of tagboard or a plain manila folder

15 to 20 pieces of origami paper or another paper of similar weight, in a variety of patterns and colors

¼-inch-wide (0.6 cm) ribbon that's not slippery (4½ feet, or 1.4 m, of ribbon makes one garland strand)

white glue

Tools

photocopier; at home, school, or the library

scissors

pencil

sewing needle with a large eye

CREATING THE TEMPLATE

1. Use a photocopier to enlarge the flower template on page 54 by 135 percent.

2. Cut out the enlarged template, and trace the shape onto a piece of tagboard or half of a manila folder. Cut out the shape.

MAKING THE FLOWERS

1. Spread the sheets of paper for the flowers on a work space, patterned or colored side down.

2. Using a pencil and the template you've cut out of tagboard or the manila folder, trace the flowers on the back of the paper. You will need from 15 to 20 flowers to create one strand of garland.

3. Cut out the flowers.

4. Curl the petals by gently running one of the blades of the scissors along the top, patterned side of each petal, much as you'd curl gift ribbon. Curl every petal of each flower.

STRINGING THE BLOOMS

1. Thread the end of the entire length of ribbon through the needle. Tie a knot at the opposite end of the ribbon.

2. To string the first flower, insert the needle through the center of the bloom, working from the back (plain) side to the front (patterned or colored) side. Gently slide the flower to the knot at the ribbon's end.

3. Apply a dot of white glue to the flower center to cover the needle hole.

4. Continue to thread the flowers, leaving about 3 inches (7.6 cm) of ribbon between each one. Glue the flowers in place as you go.

5. When you have about 6 inches (15.2 cm) of ribbon left, lay it flat on a table and allow it to dry before hanging.

MAKING A LOOP

1. When the flowers are dry, tie a knot in the last 6 inches (15.2 cm) of ribbon at the top to form a loop. You will use this to hang the finished garland on a nail or thumbtack. You can even make a curtain of garlands by hanging several of them from the top of a doorway or from the top ledge of a window.

FLOWER
TEMPLATE

Enlarge by 140 percent

PAPER CIRCLE MOBILE

This project takes a while, but it isn't difficult. And you'll have a cute mobile made from your favorite papers to decorate a corner of your room. How awesome is that?

INSPIRATION

I'm always looking for clever ways to show off my growing collection of patterned papers. One day I was surfing craft ideas on Pinterest and came across mobiles made of punched paper circles and an old wire frame from a lampshade. I had a "lightbulb!" moment. I would make my own funky, colorful mobile. I used a few papers from my coveted stash, and I also mixed in snippets from old calendars, magazine covers, greeting cards, and postcards.

PAPER CIRCLE MOBILE HOW-TO

You Will Need

1 embroidery hoop or a round wood picture frame (sample hoop is 10 inches, or 25.4 cm, across, but smaller or larger hoop would work too)

2 to 3 yards (1.8 to 2.7 m) ⅝-inch (1.6 cm) decorative ribbon

heavier weight scrap paper in a variety of colors and patterns, such as old calendars, magazine covers, postcards, greeting cards, and heavier handmade papers

7 to 10 lace-weight strands of yarn (1-yard, or 0.9 m, each) in a neutral color such as beige

2 strands (24-inch, or 61 cm) of decorative ribbon or rickrack (can be the same ribbon used to wrap the hoop)

Tools

scissors

2.5-inch (6.4 cm) and 1.5-inch (3.8 cm) hole punches

1 glue stick

1 hook to hang mobile

MAKING THE MOBILE

1. Beginning anywhere on the embroidery hoop or frame, tie a double knot with the ribbon onto the frame. Wrap the ribbon all the way around the hoop or frame, overlapping the edges of the ribbon as you wrap to cover every bit of the hoop or frame. When you reach the end, tie another knot to secure the ribbon around the hoop or frame, and trim the ends of the ribbon.

2. Use both paper punches to punch the papers you have selected with 150 to 200 circles in whatever mix of sizes you want.

3. Cut 7 to 10 strands of lace-weight yarn, 3 feet (0.9 m) each.

4. Beginning 3 inches (7.6 cm) from one end of a strand of yarn, attach the punched circles. Place one circle right side down on the worktable.

5. Apply a thin layer of glue. Place the strand of yarn across the center of the circle. Align another circle of the same size on top of the glue circle, right side up, covering the strand of yarn. Press the circles together firmly.

EMBELLISH!

If you're feeling that your mobile could use a little something extra, consider tying a few 3-foot (0.9 m) strands of pom-pom fringe or rickrack to the hoop or frame. Mix up the colors, and space the strands evenly between the circle strands.

6. Leaving about 1 inch (2.5 cm) between circles, glue circles to the strand until about 10 circles line it. Alternate circle sizes, papers, and colors to add interest. Attach the last pair of circles on the end of the strand.

7. When each strand is finished, begin a new one, until you have 7 to 10 strands of circles.

8. One by one, tie the strands to the hoop or frame with a double knot. Arrange them around the hoop or frame however you like.

9. To hang the mobile, cut two lengths of coordinating decorative ribbon or rickrack, each one 24 inches (61 cm) long. Tie the ends of each length to the hoop or frame directly across from each other. Think of the numbers on the clock, tying the ends of one ribbon at 6 and 12 and the ends of the other ribbon at 3 and 9. Bring the strands together above the hoop or frame. Adjust so it hangs straight. Wrap the centers of the two strands together to form a loop. Hang it from a hook on the ceiling or shelving so the mobile can sway gently.

HAND-CUT SNOWFLAKES

These are giant versions of the paper snowflakes you may have folded and snipped in elementary school. They look awesome hanging in a window throughout the winter season.

INSPIRATION

There is something magical about the first snowfall of winter. If I can't be out walking in the snow, I always find myself gazing out the window, watching the flakes swirl and tumble as they fall to the earth. A couple of winters ago, I thought it would be festive to hang giant snowflakes in our dining room windows. I checked stationery stores (too expensive) and a discount store (not available). Then I had a blinding flash of the obvious: "They are cut paper, so why don't we make them ourselves?" So that's just what we did. Our family spent most of an afternoon, hunched over folded poster board snowflakes-in-the-making, cutting intricate designs with craft knives and adding details with drills. Yes, you read that right, drills. If you have access to one and an adult to help you, drilling holes into the paper adds a delicate design element to these flakes. Let it snow!

HAND-CUT SNOWFLAKE HOW-TO

You Will Need

1 white tagboard, 24-inch (61 cm) × 36-inch (91.4 cm), 12 point thickness

cotton twine, string, sewing thread, or thin yarn for hanging the snowflakes

Tools

ruler or yardstick
pencil
scissors
iron and ironing board
1 piece of thick cardboard, 24 inches (61 cm) square
craft knife
drill and small drill bits (optional)
1 needle

FOLDING THE PAPER

1. Use a ruler, pencil, and scissors to cut tagboard into a 24-inch (61 cm) square.

2. Fold the tagboard in half from top to bottom. Then fold it in half again from right to left. Use a ruler to crease the folds. Do not unfold.

3. Fold in half diagonally by bringing the bottom right and top left corner together. This will create a crease through the middle of the paper and form a triangle. Fold the triangle in half diagonally again so that the bottom left and bottom right

corners come together. This will make another crease through the middle of the triangle.

4. Set up an ironing board, and preheat the iron to a low setting. When the iron is warm, press the folded triangle flat. (Don't unfold it yet.) Unplug the iron.

CUTTING THE PAPER

1. Cut the outside edge of the wide part of the triangle so that all the layers are even and none extend beyond the others.

2. Place the folded cone shape on the piece of cardboard, arranging so that the long base of the triangle is at the bottom. Beginning with the top of the triangle, use the craft knife to shape the design that will appear at the center of the snowflake. For a star-shaped center, cut a zigzag edge. For a round center, cut a curved edge. (Cut just half of each one. When you open up the paper later, the entire shape will be there.)

3. After you have cut through four or five layers, unfold one or two layers, find the imprint the blade has made on the uncut layers, and press over them again with the craft knife to cut through the paper.

4. Use the craft knife or scissors to trim a decorative edge (zigzags or curves) along the very outside edge, or widest part, of the triangle.

5. Bit by bit, cut diamonds, triangles, rectangles, and other shapes into the folded triangle, working your way around all sides. Again, when you've cut through a few layers, open the folds to work directly on areas that have an imprint of the shape you're cutting but have not yet been penetrated with the craft knife.

6. If you have a drill, you can insert the narrowest drill bit into the drill. Then drill several small holes into your design.

7. Open the folds to look at the snowflake. If you want to add more shapes, refold and cut the design you want.

8. When you are happy with how the snowflake looks, unfold the snowflake. Heat the iron again. Lightly iron over the entire snowflake to flatten it and smooth out all the fold lines.

9. Find a drill hole along the outside edge of the snowflake—or make one by pushing a needle through the paper. Thread a 12-inch (30.5 cm) length of twine, string, thread, or yarn through the hole, and tie a double knot to secure it. Hang the snowflake in a window or on a wall. Surprise friends with snowflakes on their locker!

RECYCLED PAPER JOURNAL

Made with cast-off polka-dot wrapping paper, flowers cut from last year's calendar, and a red, rickrack bookmark, this journal has become one of my favorite things. Not only is it a place to write down thoughts and feelings, it's a handmade treasure that combines reusable things I love. Think of this as an opportunity to make the journal your own—draw, write, paint, and recycle. All have a place in this portable, personal project.

INSPIRATION

No doubt about it, this project was inspired by the artwork in my Paper Source calendar for the month of May 2015. These black-and-white flowers, accented with a pop of color here and there, made me happy every time I gazed at them. So I saved them. When I was ready to make this journal, I carefully cut out a few of my favorites and began moving them around on a piece of blue-and-white polka-dot wrapping paper. (Did I mention I'm a pushover for polka dots?) Soon I found a layout arrangement that made me swoon. I knew I wanted to add a ribbon bookmark of some sort too. The coral red in the center of one of the flowers caught my eye. In my tin of ribbons and trims, I found a spool of rickrack in that very hue. It became the color I used for the inside covers as well.

● RECYCLED PAPER JOURNAL HOW-TO

You Will Need
1 sheet of patterned paper, large enough to cover the entire
   outside of the journal
1 paperback or hardcover journal or small school notebook (with
   a flat, glued spine, not a spiral notebook) with blank pages (the
   size in the sample was 6 inches × 8 inches, or 15.2 cm × 20.3 cm
2-ounce (57 g) container of Mod Podge
12 inches (30.5 cm) of ribbon or rickrack in a color of your choice
favorite photos, drawings, or other paper memorabilia (such as
   ticket stubs, postcards, or birthday cards)
2 sheets of solid color paper (8½ inches × 11 inches, or 21.6 cm ×
   27.9 cm) for the inside flaps

Tools
plastic cloth or oilcloth for your work space
ruler
pencil
scissors
1-inch (2.5 cm) paintbrush
craft knife (optional)
rock or paperweight

COVERING THE JOURNAL

1. Find a place where you are able to leave your journal to dry and it won't be moved or in the way of other people or pets. Cover the work space with a plastic cloth or oilcloth that won't stick to your journal as you work.

2. Lay out the sheet of paper you have chosen as the background layer for the front and back of the journal, print or color side down. Center your journal on top of the paper, and open the journal. Use the ruler and pencil to measure 2 inches (5.1 cm) out from the journal on all sides.

3. Close the book, and wrap the paper around the front cover, taking care not to fold or rip the paper. Check to see that the pattern of the paper aligns properly on the front and back of the book. Lay the paper and the journal back onto your work surface. Open the journal, and use a pencil to trace the outline of the book on the sheet of background layer paper.

4. Set the book aside. Use a ruler to measure 1 inch (2.5 cm) out from the top, sides, and bottom of the traced outline of the book. Make small marks with a pencil around the entire book to create a dotted line 1 inch from the border of your book outline. Then use the ruler and pencil to align and connect the 1-inch marks all around the book. This is the edge that will wrap into the back and front covers of the book.

5. Cut along the 1-inch (2.5 cm) border line you've just created.

6. Close the book, and use a paintbrush to apply a thin, even layer of Mod Podge to the back outside cover of the journal.

7. With the paper on the table and the marked inside outline of the book faceup, carefully align the back cover of the book with the traced pencil outline of the back cover.

8. Turn the book and the paper over to rest on the front cover. Carefully smooth out any wrinkles in the paper on the book's back side. Let it dry overnight.

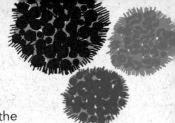

9. The next day, apply a thin, even layer of Mod Podge to the book's spine and front cover.

10. Carefully roll the book onto the spine part of the paper. Smooth any wrinkles before rolling the book over to rest on the paper for the front cover. Make sure to align the book with the pencil outline on the paper.

11. Turn the book to rest on the back cover, and carefully smooth out any wrinkles on the front. Allow to dry overnight.

FOLDING THE EDGES

1. Use a craft knife to trim off excess paper along the top and bottom of just the spine of your journal.

2. Beginning with the inside back cover of the journal, apply a thin 1-inch (2.5 cm) border of Mod Podge along the top, side, and bottom of the inside cover.

3. Carefully fold over the outer edge of paper from the back side of the notebook to cover the glue on the inside back cover. Put a dab of Mod Podge on the inside corners. Then fold the paper onto the dab of Mod Podge from one edge first and then the other.

4. Smooth out any wrinkles in the paper. Prop the back inside cover open, using something heavy, such as a rock or paperweight on the center of the back inside cover. Allow to dry overnight.

5. Repeat steps 2 to 4 to complete the inside front cover. Allow to dry overnight.

ATTACHING THE RIBBON

1. Use a paintbrush to apply a thin, even line of Mod Podge to the inside back cover of the book right along the spine, extending down from the top of the book about 2¼ inches (5.7 cm).

2. Press one end of the ribbon (or rickrack) into the Mod Podge to secure. The rest of the ribbon will hang outside the top of the journal until the glue is dry. Then it can eventually be folded into the pages of the journal to mark your place.

3. Rest a rock or paperweight on the inside of the back cover to prop it open while the ribbon dries overnight.

ADDING DECORATIVE DETAILS

1. Choose the paper elements you will use to decorate the front of your journal. Cut them out or trim them, if necessary, to fit on the cover. Then take some time to play with the arrangement of the pieces on the front cover, moving them around or layering them, or both until you like how the pieces look together.

2. Add one or more dynamic elements to your design at the spine.

3. Apply a thin, even layer of Mod Podge to cover the area where you will be placing your first element. Adhere the piece to the glue, and smooth out any wrinkles.

4. Continue to glue on each element, building on the design as you go. When you've finished the front cover, allow it to dry overnight.

5. Finish the spine and back cover just as you did the front. Allow to dry overnight.

6. Open the book, and place it flat on your work surface, inside pages facedown. Brush a thin coat of Mod Podge over the entire front cover, back cover, and spine of the journal to seal your work. Let the book dry overnight.

PAPERING THE INSIDE COVERS

1. The solid-colored pieces of paper decorate the inside covers of the book. Each one will overlap the edge of the background paper that you've already folded and glued into place. Allow for a ½-inch (1.3 cm) space between the outside edge of the solid paper and the outside edge of the book. Then a strip of background paper will show to contrast with the inside cover

paper. Trim the colored pieces of paper to the size that will work for the inside covers of your book.

2. Apply a thin, even layer of Mod Podge to the back inside cover where the solid paper will go, and carefully set the paper onto the glued surface. Smooth any wrinkles, and allow to dry overnight.

3. Repeat step 2 to cover the inside front cover. You are ready to start writing in your journal—or to gift it to a friend!

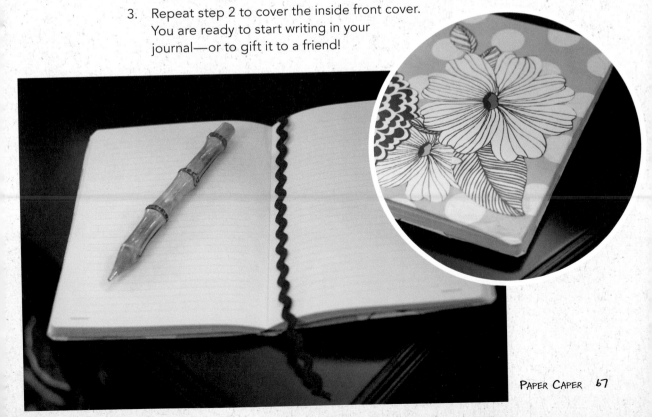

CHAPTER 3
T-SHIRT REVOLUTION

I'm always on a quest for the perfect T-shirt, one that fits just right, has a flattering neckline, and isn't too long or too short. For a long time, I picked classic white or black. Now I'm all about patterns, mostly stripes (although I'd prefer polka dots). I have a lot of T-shirts, and once a year, I purge. Sometimes I load them into bags and haul them to the thrift store. But lately, I've been finding other uses for those old T-shirts. In this chapter, you'll find a sampling of the ideas for adding new life to an old T-shirt or making something completely different from it.

APPLIQUÉD T-SHIRT

This is the perfect way to show off a favorite character, animal, design, or doodad. I used a striped T-shirt. You can use a solid T-shirt for heightened contrast, if you prefer.

INSPIRATION

I was so inspired by the idea of breathing new life into an old T-shirt that I made two, one with bikes and one with an octopus. A little serendipity was involved. I had set aside a stack of striped T-shirts of different colors because I was kicking around the idea of doing a different project with them. Meanwhile, though, I had just bought a set of sheets in a turquoise bicycle print, which came in a matching bag. This first T-shirt was a bit of a learning experience. The fabric was somewhat slippery, and the edges frayed easily, so it was hard to work with. Be sure to pick a sturdy, woven cotton fabric for this project.

Then I noticed that the orange striped T-shirt from my pile looked supercute with the blue-and-orange octopus fabric I had in my scrap bin. I love second chances! This time, I followed all the steps I'd wished I'd taken with the bicycle shirt. It turned out beautifully. So, so cute, and it's so satisfying to learn from mistakes.

APPLIQUÉD T-SHIRT HOW-TO

You Will Need
1 T-shirt, striped, patterned, or plain
1 piece of iron-on, tear-away stabilizer
1 design element cut from a piece of your favorite fabric
1 small container fabric glue (optional)
thread to match the T-shirt

Tools
iron and ironing board
scissors
straight pins
sewing machine

PREPARING THE T-SHIRT

1. If the T-shirt is new, wash and dry it to remove manufacturer's sizing chemicals and to avoid shrinkage later on.

2. Set up the ironing board, and preheat the iron on the cotton setting.

3. Cut a piece of stabilizer slightly larger than the design element you will be sewing to the T-shirt.

4. Lay the T-shirt front side down on the ironing board, smoothing away any wrinkles and aligning seams.

5. Lift the back of the shirt, and slide the iron inside to warm the inside front of the shirt.

6. Arrange the piece of stabilizer to cover the inside of the area where you will be appliquéing the design. Make sure to place the stabilizer with the shiny side down.

7. Iron the stabilizer in place, working back and forth three or four times with the hot iron.

PREPARING THE DESIGN ELEMENT

1. Cut out the design element that you would like to appliqué. Trim all edges neatly.

2. Lay the T-shirt front side up on your work surface, smoothing any wrinkles and aligning seams, as needed.

3. If your design has a lot of edges or corners or swirly shapes, it will require a lot of sewing. So use fabric glue to adhere your design to the T-shirt before pinning. Test the glue first to make sure it works with the materials you are using. Cut a piece from the design element fabric, and use a few dabs of glue to attach it to a scrap piece of T-shirt that is similar to the one you are using for this project. Be sure the colors don't bleed and the glue cannot be seen on the front side of the T-shirt fabric.

4. Apply a few small dabs of glue to the corners of the back of your design and a couple of dabs in the center. Carefully turn the design over, and place it, glue side down, on the front of the T-shirt in the area where you applied the stabilizer, smoothing edges and wrinkles. Allow the glue to dry for a few hours or overnight.

5. The next day, use straight pins to tack down the corners of the design to the T-shirt, taking care not to pin the back side of the T-shirt.

SEW!

1. Thread the sewing machine with a thread that matches the color of the design or T-shirt. Use a bobbin wound with a neutral color thread, or wind it with the same color thread you are using to sew the T-shirt. Set the machine to zigzag stitch, making sure all tension settings match what is recommended in the sewing machine manual.

2. Place the T-shirt on the bed of the machine, front side up. Align the presser foot along the very edge of the design element, so that the needle will zigzag back and forth between the design fabric and the T-shirt itself. Let down the presser foot and sew slowly, stopping to manually crank the wheel that controls the needle around tricky areas and tight corners. Remove straight pins as you approach them.

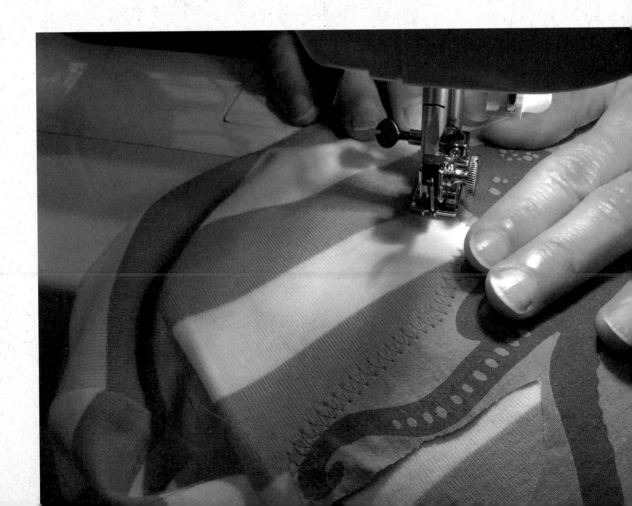

CRAFT HACK

To turn a corner when you are sewing with a sewing machine, crank the wheel by hand for the last few stitches before the turn, stopping when the needle is in the fabric, not above it. Then lift the presser foot, turn the fabric in the direction you will be sewing, and set the presser foot back down before continuing to sew.

3. Once you've stitched all the way around the design, continue stitching for four or five stitches to secure the seam. Lift the needle and the presser foot, gently pull the fabric away from the machine, and clip the threads.

4. Examine your work. If there are any areas where the design is not firmly attached to the T-shirt, you may want to resew them or make another complete pass around the design.

5. Turn the T-shirt inside out, and carefully trim away any excess stabilizer. Any remaining bits of stabilizer will gradually fall away from the fabric with repeated washings.

EMBROIDERED T-SHIRT

I went through a phase where I was doing a lot of embroidery. I loved how I could embellish a dishtowel or bag with a few colorful flowers and breathe new life into them. So one day, I pulled out my stash of embroidery floss and needles to transform a white T-shirt into something I'd be interested in wearing again. It worked!

INSPIRATION

I was browsing through the craft section at my local library one day when I came across a beautiful embroidery book. The cover of the book, *Artfully Embroidered: Motifs and Patterns for Bags and More* by Naoko Shimoda, was a field of wildflowers. It was stitched entirely in black embroidery floss. The effect was striking and elegant, and I wanted to try it myself. A white T-shirt offered the perfect canvas for my design, and I set about sketching potential flowers on paper. I transferred the design onto the T-shirt and embroidered it in black floss. I'm really happy with the result!

EMBROIDERED T-SHIRT HOW-TO

You Will Need

1 white T-shirt

1 pack 20-inch × 36-inch (50.8 cm × 91.4 cm) iron-on, tear-away stabilizer

1 to 2 skeins cotton or silk embroidery floss in any colors you want

Tools

sketchbook or scrap paper
pencil
scissors
iron-on transfer pen
iron and ironing board
embroidery hoop
embroidery needle

CREATING YOUR DESIGN

1. Lay out your T-shirt on a table or other flat surface. Study it to decide where to place the embroidered design. You can place it front and center, just below the neckline. Or you can work up from the hemline on one side of the shirt. You could even plan for a design on the back of the shirt or on the sleeves.

2. Sketch simple design ideas for your shirt on a piece of scrap paper or in a sketchbook. Remember, when you transfer your design to the T-shirt, it will be a reverse image of what you've drawn. This is especially important if you want to use words in your design. You will need to trace the letters backward to read them on the finished T-shirt. Do several sketches until you have options you like. For your first T-shirt, keep the design simple, with just one, two, or three elements.

3. Cut out your design pieces, and place them on the T-shirt to see how they look. Move the pieces around until you find the arrangement that you like best. You may decide to go with only one piece.

PREPARING THE SHIRT

1. If the T-shirt is new, wash and dry it to remove the manufacturer's sizing chemicals and to avoid shrinkage later on.

2. Use the iron-on transfer pen to trace over all elements of the design on the paper. You will transfer this to the T-shirt in step 9.

3. Cut a piece of iron-on, tear-away stabilizer large enough to cover your design.

4. Set up the ironing board, and heat the iron to the cotton setting.

5. Place the T-shirt front side down on the ironing board. Lift the back of the shirt, and slide the iron inside to warm the inside front of the shirt.

6. Arrange the piece of stabilizer to cover the inside of the area where you will be embroidering the design, making sure to place the stabilizer with the shiny side down.

7. Iron over the stabilizer several times until it is securely stuck to the shirt.

8. Flip the shirt over so that the front is facing you, smoothing and adjusting the shirt so it is straight and free of wrinkles.

9. Arrange the paper embroidery design elements where the stabilizer is, flipping them so that the ink side faces the shirt.

10. Pass the iron over each design element separately, lifting a corner to make sure the ink has adhered to the shirt after a couple of passes. If it has not, iron over the design a couple more times.

EMBROIDERING THE DESIGN

1. Slide the inner part of the embroidery hoop inside the T-shirt and under the area with the transferred design. Set the outer part of the embroidery hoop over the top of the T-shirt to cover the inner hoop. Gently squeeze together, tightening screws, if needed.

2. Pull out three threads of floss from the skein of embroidery floss, and thread them into your needle. Tie a double knot in the end of your thread. (A length of thread that matches the length of your forearm works well.)

3. My favorite all-around embroidery stitch for projects like this is the split stitch. In the sample T-shirt, I used this stitch for the outline of the flowers. **Here's how to do the split stitch:**

   a. Bring the needle up from the bottom of the fabric, pulling until the end of the thread catches at the knot.

   b. Push the needle back into the fabric ¼ inch (0.6 cm) away (rightward or leftward), following the line of the transferred pattern. Pull the thread all the way through the fabric.

   c. Insert the needle up through the fabric and through the middle of the previous stitch, piercing and separating the threads of the stitch you just made. Pull the thread all the way through.

   d. Push the needle back into the fabric ¼ inch (0.6 cm) beyond the split stitch you just made. Repeat from step 3c to continue stitching along your pattern until you are finished. Try changing floss colors for more variety!

4. Once you feel comfortable with the split stitch, you can go online to learn how to do other stitches, such as the running stitch, French knot, chain stitch, and stem stitch. One of my favorite online sites for embroidery stitches is Craftsy.com. Go to www.craftsy.com/blog/2014/04/hand-embroidery-stitches/.

5. Working from the inside of the T-shirt, insert the needle up through the fabric directly on one of the transfer lines for the design and stitch. When you get close to the end of your piece of floss, push the needle to the back side of the fabric. Slide the needle under three or four of the stitches there, tie knots to secure the thread, and snip it. Rethread your needle, and continue until you have stitched all the elements of your design.

6. Use a scissors to carefully trim any stabilizer that extends beyond the embroidered design. The remaining bits will come out eventually with washing.

RUFFLED T-SKIRT

Ruffled miniskirts were all the rage in the 1980s, and the look is popular again. Wear this skirt with leggings, a pair of flats, and a T-shirt and you're set.

INSPIRATION

A friend gave me the idea for making a ruffled skirt, but I thought it would be too difficult. Then I stumbled upon directions for making gathers in a how-to-sew-everything book. "What???" I thought to myself (or maybe I said it out loud). I couldn't believe how easy it was. So I pulled the idea out of my mental archive, dusted it off, and got to work. After conducting a little more research on Pinterest, of course. I love how it turned out!

You Will Need

3 extra-large men's T-shirts that are similar in hue or a variety of
striped T-shirts in complementary colors
1 slim-fitting stretchy skirt with an elastic waist that is the same or a
similar or complementary color as the T-shirts
thread to match T-shirts or a complementary color

Tools

tape measure
chalk
yardstick
calculator
straight pins
scissors
sewing machine
hand-sewing needle

CUTTING OUT THE RUFFLES

1. This skirt has four basic pieces—the skirt and three ruffle tiers.
   Begin by laying out all the T-shirts on your work space. Take
   time to smooth out wrinkles and align seams.

2. Use a tape measure to measure your waist, the area below your
   ribs but above your hips—pretty much right where your belly
   button is. Write down this number.

3. Lay the skirt flat on your work space, smoothing out any
   wrinkles and aligning the side seams. Use a tape measure
   to measure the width of the skirt from one side seam to the
   other. Write down the measurement, and multiply by 2. Write
   down this final answer. Then you'll be ready to make the
   ruffle tiers.

4. You will need three ruffle tiers. Try to create all the ruffle tiers using the bottom hems of the three T-shirts. Then you won't have to hem each ruffle. Measure 5 inches (12.7 cm) up from the hem at several points on the front of each T-shirt, and mark with chalk as the top of the ruffle tier. Then use a yardstick and chalk to make a horizontal line connecting the 5-inch marks from one side seam of the shirt to the other.

5. Pin just underneath the line you have drawn to keep the fabric firm. Cut out the ruffle tier along the chalk line. Cut along the side seam, and open up the piece you have cut. Measure it to see what the length is. It needs to be twice your waist measurement.

6. Set the machine to a zigzag stitch, and sew along the hemmed edge of the ruffle. Use thread that matches the color of the ruffle, or use a contrasting color to create a more decorative edge. Repeat steps 4 through 6 to make all three ruffle tiers.

SEWING THE RUFFLE TIERS

1. Set the sewing machine to a very long, loose straight stitch. Test the stitch on a scrap piece of T-shirt to make sure it is loose enough to allow you to pull the thread on the back of the scrap piece to create gathers in the material.

2. Place the first ruffle tier on the bed of the sewing machine with the top, raw edge of the long side under the presser foot. Along that edge, sew a ¼-inch (0.6 cm) seam in a loose straight stitch. When you get to the end of the piece, clip the threads at a length of 4 inches (10.2 cm).

3. Remove the ruffle tier from the machine. Pull gently on the thread on the back side of the piece to gather the ruffle. Adjust the fabric gathers evenly along the entire length of the piece so that the length of the ruffle is equal to the measurement calculated earlier in step 3 of Cutting Out the Ruffles.

4. Set the machine to a normal tighter straight stitch. Sew a ¼-inch (0.6 cm) seam along the top, gathered edge of the ruffle to secure the gathers in place.

5. Repeat this with the two other ruffle tiers.

ADDING RUFFLES TO THE SKIRT

1. Cut the skirt along one of its side seams, and lay the skirt flat on your work space with the right side faceup.

2. Measure 5 inches (12.7 cm) down from the elastic band at the waist, and mark with chalk at several points across the skirt.

3. With the wrong side of the first ruffle faceup and the zigzag hemmed edge at the top, align the gathered edge along the chalk line. Pin in place.

4. Lay the skirt on the bed of the sewing machine with pins and ruffles on top. Align the needle ⅛ inch (0.3 cm) to the right of the ruffle stitch, and sew to attach the ruffle to the skirt, removing pins as you go. Clip threads.

5. Place the skirt on the work space with the ruffle flipped up to cover the elastic band. Measure 4 inches (10.2 cm) down from the gathered-and-sewn ruffle edge, and mark with chalk at several points across the skirt. Repeat steps 3 and 4 to attach the second ruffle.

6. Repeat step 3 to 5 to sew on the third ruffle.

7. To sew the skirt's side seam together again, bring the right and left sides of the skirt toward each other. Make sure the ruffles stay on the inside of the skirt as you do this. Align and pin the skirt together to re-form the seam. Make sure to tuck ruffles away from the pins.

8. Sew a ¼-inch (0.6 cm) seam, removing pins as you go. Clip threads and turn the skirt right side out. The ruffles will naturally drop downward, right sides facing out. Try on your new skirt and take it for a spin!

STRIPED BEANIE

Hats were once a must-have part of any fashionable outfit. Nowadays, they are optional—unless it's a supercold, subzero day! But hats can be a classy accessory, adding zip and color and personality to even the most casual outfit. And if you put on a cute hat, you don't have to think about what to do with your hair!

INSPIRATION

I made this hat from a striped long-sleeved T-shirt that I loved but that never quite fit right. So I found a new way to give it some more play. The striped hat alone was a little boring. So I added the blue star. It was just the ticket, and we are all stars, right?

● STRIPED BEANIE HOW-TO

You Will Need

1 striped or colored T-shirt, short- or long-sleeved

1 solid-colored T-shirt that complements the stripes, short- or
   long-sleeved

4-inch (10.2 cm) square of felt or of an old felted sweater in a color
   that complements the stripes

1 small piece of iron-on, tear-away stabilizer

thread to match stripes or in any complementary color

Tools

tape measure

pencil, fabric marker, or white chalk

ruler or yardstick

straight pins

scissors

sewing machine

star-shaped cookie cutter (optional)

iron and ironing board

MAKING THE HAT

1. Use a tape measure to measure the circumference of your head.
    (Measure at the widest part of your head, just above your ears.)
    Write this number down. This will be the width of your hat.
    (For the sample hat, this number was 20 inches, or 50.8 cm.) If
    the fabric you are working with isn't very stretchy, add ½ inch
    (1.3 cm) to this measurement to make sure the finished hat isn't
    too tight.

2. Turn the striped T-shirt inside out, and lay it on a work space in
    front of you, smoothing out all wrinkles and aligning side seams.

3. Along the bottom seam of the shirt, use a tape measure to measure from the left side seam toward the right. Use a pencil, fabric marker, or white chalk to mark half the measurement on the shirt that you recorded for your head circumference in step 1. (For the sample hat, half the measurement was 10 inches, or 25.4 cm.)

4. Find the center point for the distance you just measured, and mark it with a straight pin. From that point, use a tape measure to measure 8 inches (20.3 cm) upward toward the neckline. Mark this top point with a pencil or other fabric marker.

5. Use a pencil or fabric marker to gently sketch an even curve from the right side of the shirt to the top center point you marked in step 4. Sketch an even curve from the top center point to the existing shirt seam on the left.

6. Make sure the back of the shirt is free of wrinkles. Pin every 3 inches (7.6 cm) all along the inside of the curved line you just drew. This will maintain the shape of the hat as you cut and sew.

7. Cut out the hat, keeping the scissors ¼ inch (0.6 cm) outside the marked line.

8. Thread the sewing machine, and set it to sew a straight stitch. Using the machine's ¼-inch (0.6 cm) mark on the bed, stitch a ¼-inch seam along the outside edge of the hat, stopping when you reach the existing side seam on the left. Turn the hat right side out.

MAKING THE BRIM

1. Lay the solid T-shirt on a work space in front of you, smoothing out all wrinkles and aligning side seams.

2. Along the bottom seam of the shirt, use a tape measure to measure from the left side seam toward the right, using a pencil to mark half the measurement you recorded for your head circumference. (For the sample hat, this measurement was 10 inches, or 25.4 cm, half of the head circumference.)

3. Measure upward from this mark 2½ inches (6.4 cm), and mark with a pencil or fabric marker. Do this again at the middle of the circumference and again at the left side.

4. Use a ruler and fabric marker to draw a horizontal line to connect the three marks you just made at 2½ inches (6.4 cm).

5. Make sure the back of the shirt is free of wrinkles. Pin along the inside of the horizontal line you just drew. Also, pin along the sides of the brim to keep the fabric firm as you cut.

6. Cut out the brim, keeping the scissors ¼ inch (0.6 cm) outside the marked lines.

7. Take out the pins, flip the brim inside out, and repin along the short right-side edge opposite the existing left-side seam.

8. Stitch a ¼-inch (0.6 cm) seam along this pinned edge. Set aside while you make the star.

SEWING ON THE STAR

1. On the square of felt or piece of sweater, draw or trace the design element you'd like to embellish on the hat. For the sample, I traced a star-shaped cookie cutter. You can find shapes online too. Print them, cut them out, and trace them onto your fabric.

2. Cut out the design.

3. Cut out a piece of stabilizer that is slightly larger than the size of your design element.

4. Set up the ironing board, and preheat the iron on the cotton setting.

5. Lay the hat with what will be the front side facing down on the ironing board. Smooth away any wrinkles and align seams.

6. Lift the back of the hat, and slide the iron inside to warm the inside front of the hat.

7. Arrange the piece of stabilizer to cover the inside of the area where you will be sewing the design, making sure to place the stabilizer shiny side down.

8. Iron the stabilizer in place, working back and forth three or four times with the hot iron.

9. Turn the hat over so the front side faces you. Align and pin the design in place, covering the area that you just backed with stabilizer and making sure you don't pin through to the back side of the hat.

10. Thread the sewing machine, and set it to zigzag stitch.

11. Adjust the front of the hat on the bed of the sewing machine so that the back side of the hat hangs down and out of the path of the needle. Align the presser foot along one of the edges of your design piece so that the needle will zigzag back and forth between the design edge and the hat itself. Let down the presser foot, and sew slowly around the edges of the design, stopping to manually crank around tricky areas and tight corners.

12. After you've stitched all the way around the design, lift the needle and the presser foot, pull the fabric away from the machine, and clip the threads.

13. Remove the pins, and examine your work. If there are any areas where the design is not firmly attached to the T-shirt hat, you may want to resew them or make another complete pass around the design.

14. Turn the hat inside out, and carefully trim excess stabilizer from around the edges.

SEWING ON THE BRIM

1. Turn the brim wrong side out, and tuck it into the inside of the hat. Align the bottom raw edge of the brim with the raw edge of the hat. Pin to attach, and sew a ¼-inch (0.6 cm) seam.

2. Pull the brim out of the hat, and turn it up. Your hat is ready to wear!

FAVORITE T-SHIRT PILLOW

T-shirts don't necessarily have to be repurposed into something you wear. Add a cozy feel to your room by making a few of these pillows. Then the design on the T-shirt that you've loved to shreds becomes a decorative feature on a pillow.

INSPIRATION

This project is a fresh twist on the old idea of making quilts from a stack of discarded, favorite T-shirts. I love quilts, especially those made from tiny squares of funky, vintage fabrics. But I have yet to see a T-shirt quilt that I really, truly love. Making a special T-shirt into a pillow covering with a brightly patterned fabric background, though, is a different story. I'm crazy about this idea. In fact, I already have a small collection of T-shirts queued up, waiting to be paired with the perfect fabric and made into pillows. Ready, set, go!

● FAVORITE T-SHIRT PILLOW HOW-TO

You Will Need

1 T-shirt with a design pattern you love that can be cut out easily

1 piece of iron-on, tear-away stabilizer, slightly larger than the size
of the design

1 lightweight kitchen towel or a piece of scrap fabric

1 pillow of any size and any filling (feather, cotton, or polyester),
either from around the house or new from a fabric store

fabric that coordinates with the T-shirt design and is the same type of
material (such as cotton), enough to cover your pillow on both sides

thread to match the T-shirt or background fabric

Tools

scissors
iron and ironing board
tape measure
fabric marker pen
yardstick
straight pins
sewing machine

PREPARING THE T-SHIRT

1. Cut out the design from the T-shirt and set aside.

2. Cut a piece of iron-on stabilizer large enough to cover the back
   of the T-shirt design.

3. Set up the ironing board, and preheat the iron on the cotton
   setting.

4. Place the T-shirt design facedown on the ironing board with
   the stabilizer on top, shiny side down. Cover with a lightweight
   kitchen towel or a piece of scrap fabric. Iron over it three or four
   times until the interfacing is fused to the T-shirt design.

5. Trim excess stabilizer from the edges of the design piece.

CUTTING THE PILLOW FRONT AND BACK

1. If you're using an old pillow, use a tape measure to measure the width and length of the pillow, allowing the tape measure to conform to the pillow's plump shape. Write down these measurements, and add an extra ½ inch (1.3 cm) to the height and the width to allow for the seams. Write down these measurements.

2. Iron the fabric.

3. Lay the fabric facedown on your worktable, smoothing all wrinkles from the surface.

4. On the back side of the fabric, use a tape measure and pen to mark the outline of the pillow shape, using the final dimensions you wrote down in step 1. Cut out the pillow shape. This will be the front of the pillow.

5. Measure and mark the fabric for the back of the pillow as you did in step 4. Make it as long as the piece in step 4, but add 4½ inches (11.4 cm) to the width. Cut out this piece.

6. Measure the width of the back pillow piece, and mark the center point. With a yardstick, draw a line up this center point to divide the back piece in half. Cut along the centerline, creating two pieces. Make a mark so you remember which is the center side of each piece.

SEWING THE PILLOW FRONT

1. Center and align the T-shirt design piece faceup on the right side of the fabric for the front side of the pillow. Pin into place along the edges.

2. Thread the sewing machine with a contrasting or matching thread. Set the machine to zigzag stitch.

3. Align the presser foot along one of the edges of your T-shirt design piece so that the needle will zigzag back and forth between the design edge and background pillow fabric. Let down the presser foot, and sew slowly around the edges of the design, stopping to manually crank around tight corners. Stitch all the way around the T-shirt design.

4. Snip threads and remove pins.

SEWING THE PILLOW BACK

1. Fold over the centerline of each of the two back pieces by ¼ inch (0.6 cm). Use a hot iron to press the crease in place. Then fold that piece under again by another ¼ inch, and press with a hot iron again.

2. When you have pressed both centerlines, sew a ⅛-inch (0.3 cm) seam along each one.

3. Lay the two back pieces on a work surface in front of you with the right sides facedown. Pull one of the center seams across the other, overlapping them by 3 inches (7.6 cm). Use two pins at the top and bottom of the center seams to tack the two back pieces together.

4. Sew a ¼-inch (0.6 cm) seam to connect the overlapping back pieces at the top and bottom of the pillow covering. Leave the center section open.

ASSEMBLING THE PILLOW

1. With the right sides facing in, align and pin the front piece to the connected back pieces, using pins along the edges to secure.

2. Sew a ¼-inch (0.6 cm) seam all the way around the edges of the pillow covering.

3. Remove pins, trim excess fabric from edges, and turn the pillow covering right side out.

4. Use a finger to push out corners, and then insert the pillow into the covering. Like it? Make another one!

CHAPTER 4

SOCK SAVVY

I had just transformed a pile of discarded striped socks into a colorful scarf when a friend regifted a bag of heavy, worn-out winter socks to me. Most people would view this gift as a burden, but I saw it as an intriguing challenge. What could I make with all those socks? I cut off the heels and feet and mixed and matched the other pieces. This chapter includes an assortment of projects you can make with all kinds of socks. Challenge yourself to see what else you can come up with!

SOCK ARM WARMERS

These easy arm warmers add a touch of whimsy and coziness to fall and winter wear. I especially like them with three-quarter-sleeve T-shirts as a colorful accessory. Make them from a single pair of knee-high socks, or mix and match with socks from different pairs that have complementary patterns and colors.

INSPIRATION

As someone who loves to bike, I'm lucky to live in an area with tons of bike trails. I begin to bike in the spring, as soon as the ice and snow and sand are cleared from the paths. I don't put my bike away until temperatures dip below freezing in the fall or early winter. I have pull-on, nylon bicycle sleeves that I can wear without a jacket. If I warm up during the ride, I can easily take off the sleeves and shove them in my back pockets, making the sleeves a much more appealing option than a bulky jacket. These sock arm warmers are a riff on the bicycle sleeves I'm so fond of. Just like their nylon counterparts, these warmers extend the biking season, making it comfortable for me to wear favorite short-sleeved or three-quarter-sleeved T-shirts well into winter. I highly recommend adding a pair or two to your wardrobe.

● SOCK ARM WARMERS HOW-TO

You Will Need
1 pair of knee-high, patterned socks or 2 pairs in a variety of
    complementary patterns and colors for mixing and matching
thread to match or complement the socks

Tools
scissors
sewing machine

DESIGNING YOUR WARMERS

1. Dump your assortment of discarded socks onto a table, and begin to look through them. Are there any that seem to go together? Or is there a pair of knee-highs that you particularly like? Set aside the appealing socks, and put the rest away.

2. Examine the socks for signs of wear and tear. If the area above the heel is worn out, for example, plan to cut off that spot and discard it.

3. Use a good, sharp scissors to cut off the heel and foot of each sock, taking care to cut in a straight line. You'll be using only the part of the sock that would ordinarily cover your leg. Set aside the "feet" for another use later.

SEWING THE WARMERS

1. Thread the sewing machine, and set the machine to a zig-zag stitch with a relatively short stitch length. Test the stitch along the cut raw edge of one of the discarded "feet" to make sure it works. The goal is to stitch ⅛ inch (0.3 cm) along the edge of each sock to create a ruffled, lettuce-edge effect. This should happen naturally as you sew the zigzag stitch along the edge. If it doesn't work, adjust the stitch length and try again. Stitching more than once over the edges won't hurt the project.

2. Once you've practiced making a lettuce edge on scraps, it's time to sew the socks. Align the raw edge under the presser foot, making sure the rest of the sock is tucked out of the way.

3. Sew the zigzag stitch all the way around the sock, directly along the edge, stitching over a few of the stitches when you reach the beginning to secure the seam.

4. Repeat steps 2 and 3 with the second sock. Your arm warmers are ready to go! For the sample warmers, I designated the ruffled edge as the elbow part and the finished cuff for the wrist. But it doesn't really matter how you wear them. Whatever feels right to you is the way to go!

STRIPY SOCK SCARF

This is a great scarf to make with the socks that didn't make it for the arm warmer craft. And if you don't have enough old socks for this project, ask your friends and family to donate their old socks!

INSPIRATION

I'm crazy for scarves. So crazy for them that I have an entire drawer devoted to them, and that drawer is usually an overflowing, tangled mess of scarves. Nonetheless, I couldn't help adding this colorful little number to my collection.

You Will Need

several pairs of striped, patterned, or solid socks of similar weight
and size, in a variety of colors, preferably thin socks in a cotton
and nylon blend to avoid too much bulk (sample is made of
24 socks)

thread to match or complement the socks

Tools

scissors

sewing machine

straight pins (optional)

MAKING THE SCARF

1. Cut heels and feet
    from socks in a
    straight, even line. Use
    only the part of the
    socks that ordinarily fit
    on your leg.

2. Arrange cut socks on
    a table or work space,
    and begin to line
    them up in a pleasing
    order. Look for similar
    or complementary
    colors and patterns.

3. Thread the sewing machine, and set the machine to a medium-length straight stitch.

4. Plan to begin and end the scarf with a cuff for a smooth, finished edge.

5. Holding the first sock with the cuff side at the top, stuff the opposite raw edge of another sock into the cuff, making sure it extends into the sock by at least ½ inch (1.3 cm). Pin together.

6. Sew a ¼-inch (0.6 cm) seam along the top of the cuff of the second sock. Be sure to sew through all the layers of the two socks.

7. Repeat steps 5 and 6, adding another sock to the previous sock, and so on.

8. When the scarf is the desired length, attach the final sock. Turn the final sock inside out, and slide it (cuff first) over the unfinished end of the scarf. Align the two raw edges, and sew a ¼-inch (0.6 cm) seam. Turn the final sock right side out. Your scarf is ready to wear!

SOCK-IT-TO-'EM PHONE COZY

Believe it or not, a sock makes the perfect protective sleeve for a smartphone. And it's easy and quick to sew. If pom-pom trim isn't your thing, omit it or replace it with another embellishment. Consider rickrack, striped ribbon, fringe, beads, or buttons.

INSPIRATION

One fall day, I leaned over to pick up a pencil I had dropped on the back patio. My phone tumbled from my front pocket and onto the hard bricks below. Yes, the screen on my phone shattered into a spiderweb of cracks. It made for a festive look in the weeks just before Halloween, but it was no treat to pay to have the screen replaced. I found the answer in my bag of socks. I loved the colors in this sock and the variation in the width of the stripes. I pulled out my box of ribbons and trims, spotted the tiny gray pom-pom fringe, and I was sold. I had the makings of a new phone cozy right at my fingertips.

You Will Need

1 pair medium-weight ribbed socks in a pattern or color you like
thread to match or complement the socks
5 inches (12.7 cm) of trim of your choice (optional)
1 small square Velcro, roughly 1 inch × 1 inch (2.5 cm × 2.5 cm)
thread to match Velcro

Tools

scissors
tape measure
straight pins
sewing machine
sewing needle

SIZING THE COZY

1. Cut off the foot of each sock, just above the heel. Keep the feet.

2. Turn the leg of one sock inside out, and slide your phone into
    it to check the fit. The sock ribbing will serve as the bottom of
    the cozy. If the sides are not snug, pinch the amount of excess
    sock and pin to fit tightly. For reference, the main sleeve of the
    sample phone cozy measures 2¾ × 5½ inches (7 cm × 14 cm).
    Size will vary depending on the phone.

3. Thread the sewing machine. Set the machine to straight stitch.

4. Sew a seam along the line you pinned to take in the excess
    sock. Trim off any excess sock to remove bulk.

MAKING THE TOP FLAP

1. Cut off the top panel (the part of the sock that covers the top of the foot) from each sock's foot. Place the right sides together to form the top flap of the phone sleeve. For reference, the top flap of the sample measures 2½ inches (6.4 cm) wide by 4 inches (10.2 cm) long.

2. If you are using trim, cut the piece of trim in half, so you have two pieces measuring 2½ inches (6.4 cm) each.

3. Arrange the stacked pieces for the top flap on your work space with the shorter sides at the top and bottom. Starting at the top, pull the first layer of the flap toward you. Place the flat, ribbon edge of a piece of trim along the shorter (2½-inch, or 6.4 cm), top edge. Roll back the top layer of the flap (right side down). The pom-pom trim should be tucked inside, between the two fabric layers.

4. Pin to secure the trim. Also, pin together each of the two long (4-inch, or 10.2 cm) sides of the flap.

5. Sew a ¼-inch (0.6 cm) seam up one 4-inch (10.2 cm) side, across the 2½-inch (6.4 cm) side with the pom-pom trim, and down the other 4-inch side. Turn the flap right side out.

SEWING THE MAIN SLEEVE

1. Leave the main sleeve of the cozy inside out. Along the short-side edge with ribbing, tuck in the remaining strand of pom-pom fringe, adjusting so that the flat ribbon edge aligns with the top of the ribbing and the pom-poms are covered in the pocket. Pin in place.

2. Sew a ¼-inch (0.6 cm) seam along the top ribbing edge.

3. On the opposite short-side edge of the main sleeve, turn down the raw edge and sew a ¼-inch (0.6 cm) seam along the front side of the cozy. Leave the back side of the top unfinished. Flip the main sleeve right side out.

ATTACHING THE TOP FLAP

1. With the flap right side out, align the bottom edge of the top flap with the top back edge of the main sleeve. Pin together the raw edges of each bottom layer. Note: The top flap and main sleeve are each pockets. Store a cash card in the top flap pocket and your phone in the main sleeve.

2. Sew a ¼-inch (0.6 cm) seam to connect the flap to the top back edge of the bottom sleeve. Make sure to sew only through one layer of fabric on each piece.

ATTACHING THE VELCRO STRIP

1. Place your phone in the main sleeve, close the top flap, and decide where to put the Velcro strip. Attach the Velcro to the back of the top flap and the front of the main sleeve. Make sure they align.

2. Use a needle and thread to tack down each edge of Velcro.

SOCKADELIC MITTS

The transformation of socks into mittens is almost effortless. The cuff of the socks easily becomes the cuff of the mittens. And there are hardly any seams to sew. So easy and so fun!

INSPIRATION

Sometimes the elements of a project come together easily, almost as if they are conspiring to tell you what to make with them. That's exactly what happened when I pulled a pair of olive-and-cream snowflake-patterned socks from my sock stash. They immediately reminded me of Nordic mittens, so that's what they became. Combined with a multipatterned maroon-and-tan pair, I shaped the socks into a pair of cozy mittens.

● SOCKADELIC MITTS HOW-TO

You Will Need

1 to 2 pairs of thick, warm socks in complementary patterns and colors
thread to match or complement the socks

Tools

scissors
tape measure
pencil
straight pins
sewing machine

CUTTING OUT THE PIECES

1. Arrange the socks on a work space in front of you. Think about how you'd like to design your mittens. Which pair of socks would you like to use as the cuff and body of your mitts? Note that the leg and cuff of that pair become the body of the mittens. Which pair for the complementary thumbs? You will use the top of the sock feet of the other pair for them. Select two pairs of socks to work with.

2. Cut the feet from both pairs of the socks, trimming in a straight, even line just above the heel. Keep the feet from the socks. The tops of the feet will become the mitten thumbs.

3. Measure the distance from 2 inches (5.1 cm) below the base of your wrist up to the middle knuckle of your middle finger. Write down the measurement.

4. On one of the socks from which you cut off the heel, measure down from the edge of the cuff the same number of inches you measured in step 3. Mark this spot with a pin. Repeat this step with the other sock for the body of the mitten. Then cut across the top of the two socks at this marked spot, trimming in a straight, even line.

5. Place the body of the mitts that you just cut onto the work space in front of you. Place the cuffs at the bottom. Align two other socks above them, with the cuffs at the top. Trim off the cuffs of the top socks, rounding the corners for a curved shape. These will be the tops of the mittens.

6. Place the feet you cut from the socks for the thumbs on the work space. Use a sharp pair of scissors to cut the top panel from each foot. These will become the mitten thumbs.

SEWING THE MITTENS

1. Flip the mitten tops inside out (with right sides facing each other).

2. Thread the sewing machine, and set the machine to straight stitch.

3. Sew a ¼-inch (0.6 cm) seam along the curve of each mitten top, sewing the two layers together.

4. Study the mitten bodies to figure out which side will face the palm and which will face the front of the hand. This was an easy decision on the sample mittens, because there was a seam on the body of the mitts. I decided the seam would be on the palm side.

5. With the mitten tops and bodies inside out, align the top of each mitten along the top edge of the mitten bodies. Pin into place, and sew a ¼-inch (0.6 cm) seam around the perimeter of the mitten. Be careful not to stitch the top of the mitten closed. Stitch over a few of the stitches as you finish, to secure the seam.

6. Fold each thumb in half from right to left so that the right sides of the fabric face each other. Try the thumb on for fit. It should fit snugly without being too tight.

7. Sew a ¼-inch (0.6 cm) seam around the open side of each thumb.

8. Turn the mittens right side out, and try on one of them. Use a fabric pen to mark the spot where the base of your thumb starts. Remove the mitt, and use the scissors to make a small snip at the spot you marked. This is where you will sew on the fabric for the thumb. Repeat this step with the other mitten.

9. Turn the thumbs right side out. Slide the thumb through the thumbhole. You may need to snip a slightly larger hole, but be careful. If the hole is too large, you'll have more sewing to do to close it up.

10. Make adjustments to each thumb, as needed. Turn the thumb's seam so it aligns with the outside edge of the thumb for comfort. And if the base is too long, trim it. Then carefully turn the mittens inside out. Don't pull out the thumbs. Pin the raw edges of the thumbs on the inside of the mitten.

11. Position the thumb on the bed of the sewing machine so that the raw edges of the mitten and thumb are layered beneath the presser foot. Make sure the opposite side of the thumb is tucked away from the needle. Slowly working your way around the perimeter of the thumb, sew a ¼-inch (0.6 cm) seam. Stop as needed to readjust the layers of the thumb and mitten edges. Turn right side out, and check your work. Resew seams, if needed. Trim excess fabric along seam lines as needed, taking care not to cut the seam itself. Repeat with the second mitten. Turn the mittens right side out, and you're ready to go!

CHAPTER 5

OLD SWEATER MADE NEW

What could possibly be inspiring about an old sweater? you ask. If you're anything like me, there's a good chance that sweater has been spending a lot of time in the back of your dresser drawer. Maybe you've decided you don't really like the color or the pattern. Or perhaps the sweater is just too big and boxy or too snug.

This chapter is all about what happens next. By making the decision to reuse something you're no longer wearing, you've opened the door to new ideas. This is the moment in which creative inklings spark. You can begin to look at that sweater in a whole new way. This chapter includes a few options for giving an old sweater new life. Sweaters come in all shapes, colors, and styles. What do you see when you look at your sweater?

PATCHWORK SCARF

This scarf has all the elements of a perfect gift—it's handmade, cute, and snuggly. Best of all, it's quick to make. So quick, you may just want to make one for yourself while you're at it.

INSPIRATION

For a few years, my absolute favorite sweater was a plain gray T-shirt-style cashmere number with rolled hems. I loved it so much that I wore it to shreds, literally. I had a big hole in one of the elbows and a tear in an underarm. Finally, I realized it was time to remove it from my sweater drawer. But I couldn't let it go completely, so I stacked it in a basket with some other sweaters I'd collected for projects. At one point, the gray sweater was sandwiched between an orange cashmere cardigan, a light blue cardigan, a light blue-and-white striped pullover, and a men's gray-on-gray Fair Isle pullover. I suddenly saw that I had a scarf in the making!

PATCHWORK SCARF HOW-TO

You Will Need
assortment of 3 to 5 very soft sweaters
thread in a complementary color
yarn in a complementary color

Tools
sheet of newspaper
pencil
ruler
scissors
straight pins
sewing machine
embroidery needle

CUTTING THE SCARF PIECES

1. The first step is to create a template. On a sheet of newspaper, use a pencil and ruler to measure and draw a 7¼ × 6¼-inch (18.4 cm × 15.9 cm) rectangle. Cut out the template and set aside.

2. Arrange your sweaters front side up on a large worktable, pulling the sleeves out to the sides. Smooth the surface of the sweaters, making sure that the front and back sides are completely flat, with no wrinkles. Make sure the side seams (if any) are aligned along the outer edge.

3. Look for details in your sweaters that will make nice end pieces for your scarf.

4. Use pins to attach the template to the piece of the sweater you've chosen as one of the end pieces for your scarf. Align the template so that stripes or patterns are even. Cut out the sweater piece along the template's outer edge.

5. Repeat step 4 for the other end piece for your scarf.

6. Continue cutting out pieces from the rest of your sweaters until you have approximately 10 rectangles for your scarf. (The sample scarf uses two rectangles from each of five sweaters. You can use fewer or more sweaters, depending on what you have to work with.)

ASSEMBLING THE SCARF

1. Prepare the sewing machine with thread that matches or complements the sweater pieces.

2. Decide how you would like to arrange the rectangles of your scarf. Then stack the first rectangle (one of the end pieces) on top of the second one, with wrong sides facing each other. You will sew the pieces together along the 7¼-inch (18.4 cm) sides. Sew a ¼-inch (0.6 cm) seam along that side of the first two fabric pieces.

3. Work your way through the rectangles of fabric, adding one piece at a time to the unsewn edge of the scarf and stitching the pieces together until you have one piece left.

4. To finish, sew on the rectangle you have chosen as the other end of your scarf.

EMBELLISH!

If you like, you can embellish the edges of the scarf all the way around, using the blanket stitch in a contrasting color yarn. **Here's how to do a blanket stitch:**

1. Thread a needle with a length of yarn about the length of your forearm. Tie a knot at the end. Insert the needle up through the scarf, about a ¼ inch (0.6 cm) from the edge you're embellishing, and pull up on the thread until you feel the knot catch at the end.

2. Pull the yarn over the edge of the fabric to the underside of the scarf, and push the needle up through the same hole in step 1. You have just made a loop around the edge of the fabric.

3. Working from the top of the fabric, slide the needle along the edge of the fabric from left to right and through the loop you just made. This anchors the stitch.

4. To make the next stitch, insert the needle from the top of the fabric about ¼ inch (0.6 cm) to the right of the stitch you just made. Pull the thread almost all the way through the fabric. Then bring your needle back up through the fabric. Thread your needle left to right through the small loop of thread lying across the top of the fabric and pull tight.

5. Repeat step 4, working your way around the bottom edge of the scarf.

6. When you reach the first stitch, complete your work by sliding your needle underneath the first stitch. Then insert your needle from the top of the fabric down through the first hole of the first stitch. Tie the yarn in a double knot to secure, and snip the end of the yarn.

WOOLY TABLET COVER

This looks like a complicated project with lots of steps. But it's actually pretty easy—and quicker to make than you'd think. It makes a perfect grab-and-go protection for your tablet. Embellish with buttons, rickrack, ribbon, or flowers to give it your signature style.

INSPIRATION

True confession. On a visit to my mother's home, I raided her abundant stash of old wool sweaters. It's a collection she has carefully culled over countless trips to the local thrift store. I wanted to make a couple of tablet covers. So she and I sat down and made them right on the spot. It was a perfect mother-daughter project! Try it with your mother, or invite a friend to make some with you.

WOOLY TABLET COVER HOW-TO

You Will Need

1 size large or extra-large sturdy wool sweater, felted [see p. 120 for instructions on how to felt a sweater]

thread in a color that matches the sweater

1 length of leather shoelace or thin, sturdy ribbon or string, 3 inches (7.6 cm) long

1 large button with two holes

Tools

scissors

tape measure or yardstick

pencil or marking chalk

straight pins

sewing machine

sewing needle

CUTTING THE COVER

1. Arrange the sweater front side up on your work space. Smooth the sweater's surface, making sure that the front and back sides are completely flat with no wrinkles. Align the side seams (if any) along the outer edges of the sweater.

2. Cut along each of the side seams of the sweater, beginning at the bottom hem, working around the inside seam where the sleeve meets the body of the sweater. Continue cutting along the shoulder, through the neckline, and across the other shoulder. You will have two sweater pieces, one front and one back.

3. Place both pieces of the sweater on your work surface, right side up. Study the patterns in the sweater, and decide on an area in one of the pieces that you'd like to use for the tablet cover. (You won't need the second piece for this project; set it aside for another craft.)

HOW TO FELT A SWEATER

Felting a sweater is simple. You wash it in hot, soapy water to make the individual fibers shrink and contract. When the fibers shrink, the fabric of the sweater becomes denser and the size of the sweater shrinks. A denser fabric like felted (boiled) wool is great for making projects like purses, because a denser fabric holds its shape better. This only works with sweaters that are 100 percent wool or other animal fiber. Even the smallest percentage of human-made fibers (such as nylon or acrylic) will not felt. Be sure to check the sweater label before you buy or choose a sweater for this project. Here's how to felt a sweater:

1. Turn the sweater inside out, and place it in the washing machine. Set the water temperature as hot as possible. Add a small amount of laundry detergent (¼ cup, or 62.5 g, for a single sweater or ½ cup, or 125 g, for a full load). Tip: If you have several sweaters of the same or similar color, you can wash them together to felt them at the same time. Don't wash light-colored sweaters with dark-colored sweaters. The dark colors will bleed, creating an uneven or muddy look for the light-colored sweaters.

2. Wash the sweater. Toss it into the dryer. Once the sweater is dry, check the size and density. If you'd like it to be even denser, repeat the wash cycle, drying after the wash is complete. After two cycles of washing and drying, no more felting will occur.

4. With a tape measure, measure the height and width of the tablet you'll be storing in the cover. Write down these measurements. To determine the size of the piece you will cut from the sweater, use this guide:

Height of tablet cover piece = (height of tablet × 2) + 4 inches (10.2 cm)

Width of tablet cover piece = width of tablet + 1 inch (2.5 cm)

5. Use a tape measure or yardstick, pencil or marking chalk, and straight pins to measure, mark, and pin the sweater piece according to the dimensions calculated in step 4.

6. Use a scissors to cut slightly outside the chalk line.

SEWING THE COVER

1. Arrange the pattern piece on the work space in front of you so that the long sides are on the right and left, and the right side of the fabric is faceup.

2. Use a scissors to trim the corners from the top edge of the piece, creating a rounded top. This will become the flap for the cover.

3. Thread the sewing machine with a color that matches the sweater. Set the machine to zigzag stitch. Lay the bottom edge of the piece (the edge opposite the curved top flap) on the sewing machine bed. Stitch a seam close to the edge to prevent fraying or raveling. Snip threads.

4. Turn the pattern piece around, and stitch a zigzag seam all along the top edge of the cover's curved flap, staying close to the edge of the fabric. Snip threads.

5. Again, arrange the pattern piece on the work space in front of you so that the curved flap is at the top and the right side of the fabric is faceup. Place the tablet 4 inches (10.2 cm) from the top of the pattern piece. Then lift the bottom edge of the piece, and fold it up to cover the tablet, creating an envelope.

Pull the flap down to cover the tablet. Then both the wrong side of the top flap fabric and the wrong side of the envelope fabric are facing you.

6. Lift the flap, pull out the tablet, and set the tablet aside.

7. Secure the right and left sides of the envelope with straight pins every ¼ inch (0.6 cm) or so.

8. Set the sewing machine to straight stitch. Sew a ¼-inch (0.6 cm) seam along the two sides of the envelope. Trim the threads. Turn the cover right side out.

ATTACHING THE LOOP AND BUTTON

1. Arrange the cover in front of you so that the flap is open and at the top, with the wrong side of the flap faceup.

2. Fold the leather shoelace or sturdy ribbon or string in half to create a loop. Align the two ends of the lace to overlap the top center of the flap by ½ inch (1.3 cm). This will create a loop that will extend up from the top center of the flap by about 2 inches (5.1 cm).

3. Snip a 1½-inch (3.8 cm) square piece from the leftover sweater pieces, and pin it to cover the ends of the lace. Before sewing in place, test to make sure the button fits snugly into the loop. Tighten or loosen the loop, as necessary.

4. Set the machine to straight stitch. Place the flap on the bed with the square piece faceup, and sew around all four sides of the scrap piece. Then sew back and forth across the center of the square a couple of times to secure the ends of the loop.

5. Slide the tablet into the envelope, and close the flap. Use chalk or a straight pin to mark the spot where the bottom of the loop rests on the tablet cover. This is where you will sew on the button. Remove the tablet, and set it aside.

6. Thread the needle, doubling over the thread at a length about as long as your forearm. Tie a double knot at the end of the thread.

7. To sew on the button, insert the needle from the inside of the envelope up through to the outside at the spot you marked, inserting the needle through one of the holes on the button.

8. Insert the needle down through the hole across from the first hole and through the top of the envelope.

9. Repeat, pushing the needle up through one buttonhole and down through the other four or five times or until the button is secure.

10. Pull the needle down through the top of the envelope to the inside, and tie the thread in a double knot. Trim threads.

11. Slide the tablet into the envelope, pull the loop over the button, and you're ready to go!

EMBELLISH!

Decorate your tablet cover with embroidery stitches or a felted flower. Or sew a strand of complementary colored rickrack along the inside of the bottom edge of the top flap.

JESTER'S HAT

Made with a mix of colors and patterns, this hat never fails to bring a smile. Wear it to brighten and warm the dreariest of winter days, whether you're walking to school or hitting the slopes. Or include it in your plans for this year's Halloween costume.

INSPIRATION

My mom has a jester's hat hanging in her living room that looks as if it came straight from a costume ball in New Orleans. It's made of colorful sequined fabrics, three-corner-hat style. Each corner extends out from the hat, and like an octopus's tentacle, it curls slightly at the end. From each end, a bell dangles, creating music whenever the lucky wearer moves. I think it's pretty much impossible to be unhappy wearing that hat. So I set out to make my own version. Not only did I want my hat to bring a bit of joy to whomever wears it (and to others), I wanted it to be warm as well. Go wild making this hat. Mix colors and patterns. Run stripes sideways or vertically. Add bells instead of bobbles. Experiment to make it your own.

JESTER'S HAT HOW-TO

You Will Need

3 soft sweaters in bright colors, including one with a pattern (such as striped, paisley, or polka dots)

thread in a complementary color

3 large felted bobbles (see page 150) or pom-poms (see page 154) or from a craft store in complementary colors.

1 handful of polyester fiberfill, scrap fabric, yarn, or cotton balls (optional)

Tools

tape measure
sheet of newspaper
pencil
ruler
scissors
straight pins
sewing machine
sewing needle

CUTTING THE PIECES

1. Use a tape measure to measure the circumference of your head. (Measure at the widest part of your head, just above your ears.) Divide this by 3 to calculate the width of each of the three squares that will make up the hat. You don't have to be totally precise. For example, the sample hat was made to fit a person with a 20-inch (50.8 cm) head, so each of the squares is 6½ (16.5 cm) inches wide.

2. Create a template. On a sheet of newspaper, use a pencil and ruler to measure and draw a rectangle that is 8¼ inches (21 cm) long by the measurement you calculated in step 1 for the width. Cut out the template.

3. Then cut a template from newspaper for the brim of the hat. The brim will measure the circumference of the head in length and 2½ inches (6.4 cm) in width.

4. Arrange your sweaters front side up on a large worktable, pulling the sleeves out to the sides. Smooth the surface of the sweaters, making sure that the front and back sides are completely flat, with no wrinkles. Make sure the side seams (if any) are aligned along the outer edge.

5. Look for details or colors in your sweaters that will make a nice, finished brim for the hat. The bottom ribbing of a sweater is perfect because the edge is already finished and will make for a clean, polished look. Make sure that part of the sweater is big enough to fit the template you cut in step 3.

6. Use straight pins to attach the brim template to the sweater. Cut out the brim piece along the template's outer edge.

7. Then pin the rectangular hat template onto another sweater. Cut out that piece along the template's outer edge. Repeat for the other two pieces of the hat. Remember to cut each piece from a different sweater.

ASSEMBLING THE HAT

1. Stack the first two blocks of fabric with right sides together. Along the 8¼-inch (21 cm) edge, sew a ¼-inch (0.6 cm) seam.

2. Add the third block to the unsewn 8¼-inch (21 cm) edge of one of the connected blocks, remembering to stack the third block against the second block with right sides facing together. Sew a ¼-inch (0.6 cm) seam.

3. Then you will have a three-piece scarf. Lay the scarf on a work space in front of you with the right sides facing up. Pull the fabric piece on the right side halfway across the center block, and do the same with the left side. Align the two edges of the right and left blocks together (right sides facing each other) so they overlap by ½ inch (1.3 cm) and pin. The wrong side of the

fabric will be facing you. Sew a ¼-inch (0.6 cm) seam along the final 8¼-inch (21 cm) side to connect the three sides of the hat.

4. Pin together the pieces along the top edge of the hat into three points starting where panels have already been sewn together and meeting at the center. The top of the hat will form a T shape. Sew a ¼-inch (0.6 cm) seam.

5. Turn the hat right side out, and pin the raw edge of the brim piece—wrong side facing out—along the bottom edge of the hat. To do this, align the bottom raw edge of the brim with the raw edge of the hat and tuck the rest of the brim piece into the inside of the hat. Pin to attach and sew a ¼-inch (0.6 cm) seam through the brim and the hat pieces, all the way around. Pull the brim out of the hat, and fold up along the seam you just sewed.

6. With a sewing needle and thread, sew bobbles or pom-poms to each corner of the hat.

7. Try on the hat. If your bobbles droop too much, stuff the corners of your hat with a small amount of polyester fiberfill, scrap material, or cotton balls to prop them up.

EMBROIDERED FINGERLESS MITTS

In my part of the world, when cold temperatures set in, there's nothing cozier than a soft pair of fingerless mitts to keep the chill away. Made of luxuriously soft cashmere and embellished with cheery stars, these are a perfect addition to a winter wardrobe.

INSPIRATION

Is it possible to be inspired by color alone? I think so. I fell for the dark lilac of the zip-up hoodie sweater that became these mitts the moment I saw it on the rack at my local secondhand shop. When I touched the sweater, there was no turning back—100 percent cashmere. That sweater was definitely coming home with me!

CRAFT HACK

If you ever come across 100 percent cashmere sweaters at a thrift store and the price is right, buy them. They make amazing scarves, mittens, and hats. And the material is really nice to work with.

Not long after I found the sweater, I was lucky enough to discover a stash of colorful crewel embroidery floss at an estate sale in my neighborhood. When I got home, I pulled out a few small skeins of lime green, orange, and pink and set them alongside the sweater. The match was heavenly, and all I had to do was start stitching.

● EMBROIDERED FINGERLESS MITTS HOW-TO

You Will Need
soft sweater in a color you love
thread in a color that matches or complements the color of the sweater
crewel embroidery floss in three complementary colors

Tools
tape measure
fabric pen
scissors
ruler
sewing machine
crewel embroidery needle

MAKING THE MITTS

1. Arrange the sweater front side up on a large worktable, pulling the sleeves out to the sides. Smooth the surface of the sleeves. Make sure that the front and back sides are completely flat, with no wrinkles. Make sure that the side seams (if any) are aligned along the outer edge.

2. Use a tape measure to measure from the first knuckle of your pointer finger to the middle of your forearm. This will be the length of your mitts. Write down the measurement. For reference, the sample mitts are 9¾ inches (24.8 cm) long.

3. Use the tape measure to measure from the bottom of the sweater's sleeve cuff up the sleeve the same number of inches you used in step 2. Make a small mark there with a fabric pen. Repeat for the second sleeve.

4. Use a scissors to cut off the sleeves at the points you marked, taking care to cut in a straight line.

5. Slip your hand through one of the sleeves you cut, with your fingers poking out of the top of the sleeve cuff. Adjust until comfortable. On the sample mitts, I placed the side hem on the inside.

6. Use a fabric pen to mark the spot where the base of your thumb starts. Remove the mitt, and use the scissors to make a small snip at the spot you marked. You will sew on the fabric for the thumb there.

MAKING THE THUMB

1. Along the base of the sweater's hem, use a tape measure to measure 3 inches (7.6 cm) across, marking that length with a ruler and your fabric pen. Measure up from that mark 2¾ inches (7 cm), and mark that length with a ruler and fabric pen. Cut out the marked rectangle. This will be the thumb.

2. Repeat step 1 to cut out the second thumb.

3. Fold one thumb in half so that the shorter (2¾-inch, or 7 cm) sides touch and the wrong side of the fabric (if any) faces out. Pin the shorter (2¾-inch) sides together. Thread your sewing machine with a color that matches the sweater. Sew a ¼-inch (0.6 cm) seam along the shorter side of the rectangle. Turn the thumb right side out.

4. Repeat step 3 to make the second thumb.

5. Try on the thumbs to see how they feel. Trim along the bottom raw edge if they are too long. Leave ¼-inch (0.6 cm) extra fabric for sewing the thumb to the mitt.

ADDING THE THUMBS

1. Turn one mitt inside out, and find the snip in the side. With the thumb tube right side out, insert it through the thumbholes. (You may need to use the scissors to carefully make the hole slightly larger.) Note that the thumb will be inside the mitt.

2. Align the edges of the raw base of the thumb with the edges of the mitt. Maneuver the edges beneath the presser foot of your sewing machine. Make sure the edges are aligned and no other pieces of the mitt are within reach of the needle.

3. Stitch slowly and use a straight stitch. Work your way around the thumbhole. Lift the presser foot and turn the mitt, as needed.

4. Snip threads and turn the mitt right side out. The right side of the thumb should be facing you.

5. When the thumb is complete, use the scissors to carefully snip away excess edges around the inside of the thumb. Avoid cutting the seam you just finished sewing.

6. Repeat steps 1 through 5 to sew on the second thumb.

FINISHING

1. Set the sewing machine to zigzag stitch. Adjust the thread tension and all other settings as directed in the sewing machine manual.

2. To finish the raw edge of the mitt's sleeve, zigzag stitch along the edge, all the way around the sleeve. Repeat for the second mitt.

EMBELLISH!

Using crewel embroidery yarn, you can create all kinds of designs to make the mitts your own. Here's what to do to re-create the stitching on the mitts I made:

1. Thread the embroidery needle with one of the three colors of crewel embroidery yarn. Cut the yarn to a length about as long as your forearm, and tie a double knot near the end.

2. Stitch asterisk stars here and there on the back side of your mitts (the side people will see when you're wearing them). Then add a blanket stitch (see page 117) along the edges, and add a running stitch along the middle of the mitt near your wrist. Change threads for each stitch. See instructions for the asterisk and running stitch.

Asterisk Star Stitch

Here's how to make an asterisk star stitch:

1. Insert the tip of the needle from the inside of the mitt to the outside, where you would like the center of the star to be.

2. Pull the yarn up through the mitt until you feel the knot catch at the end.

3. Insert the needle back down through the mitt about ¼ inch (0.6 cm) away from your starting point.

4. Push the tip of the needle back up through the center of the star and then down ¼ inch (0.6 cm) in the opposite direction of the first stitch.

5. Repeat, always coming up in the center and stitching out ¼ inch (0.6 cm) in a new direction until you've made a six-pointed star. When you've finished a star, pull the thread to the inside of the mitt, tie a double knot where the yarn meets the fabric, and snip off the yarn.

Running Stitch

I used this simple stitch to add a design element dividing the top of the mitt from the bottom. Thread the needle, cut to length, and tie a double knot at the end. To start the running stitch, do this:

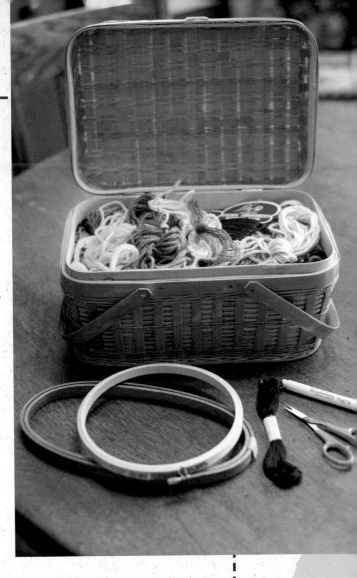

1. Insert the needle up from the underside of the fabric, and pull up on the thread until you feel the knot catch at the end.

2. Insert the needle down into the fabric about ¼ inch (0.6 cm) from the starting point. Then insert the needle back up through the fabric from the bottom side, about ¼ inch farther away.

3. Continue in this way, moving the needle down through the fabric and back up again in ¼-inch (0.6 cm) segments.

4. When you are finished, draw the needle through to the underside of the fabric, tie the end in a double knot, and snip.

FELTED PURSE WITH BOBBLES

This vintage-style purse adds the perfect pop of color to any outfit. It is made from a cast-off black wool sweater and is lined with parts from a pajama top. You can purchase bobbles at a craft store—or you can make your own by following the directions on page 150.

INSPIRATION

I once had a beautifully tailored black boiled-wool (felted) sweater with a funnel neck that fit me perfectly. I loved it and wore it often. Then, by accident, it found its way into the washing machine and then the dryer with a load of laundry. When I pulled it from the dryer, I gasped. The sweater was several sizes smaller. It may have fit my dog, but it would never again fit me. I threw it into a paper grocery bag, destined for the thrift store, and said good-bye to the sweater. But at my house, those thrift bags have a way of sitting in a corner of the basement. When I got around to sorting through the bag, I pulled out the sweater. Maybe I would make mittens from the wool and embroider them in bright colors. But then I stumbled across knitted purse patterns by Noni Designs, including one that was embellished with felted bobbles. This purse is a variation on that theme, sewn from an old sweater instead of knit from scratch.

● FELTED PURSE WITH BOBBLES HOW-TO

You Will Need
a felted black or solid-color crewneck or funnel-neck sweater,
    100 percent wool (not softer wools, such as cashmere, which
    won't hold their shape, or nonfelted, which may not hold up well)
¾ yard (0.7 m) scrap fabric for lining
thread to match the color of the liner fabric
¾ yard firm interfacing
thread to match the color of the sweater
16 to 20 felted bobbles in various sizes and colors, handmade (see
    page 150) or bought at a yarn store, craft shop, or online
40-inch (1 m) length of 1-inch (2.5 cm) pom-pom trim in a
    coordinating color

Tools
pencil
ruler, tape measure, or both
newspaper, for creating a template
scissors
straight pins
iron and ironing board
sewing machine
sewing needle

CREATING THE PURSE PATTERN PIECES

1. Arrange the sweater front side up on a large worktable. Smooth the sweater's surface, making sure that the front and back sides are completely flat, with no wrinkles. Make sure the side seams (if any) are aligned along the outer edge of the sweater.

2. Study the sweater, and consider the shape of your purse. In the sample, the bottom hem of the sweater became the top edge of the purse, allowing me to avoid sewing one more seam. (The sample purse is a half circle, measuring 13 inches, or 33 cm wide and 7 inches, or 17.8 cm, tall.)

3. Draw the half-circle shape of the purse to actual size (13 inches, or (33 cm, wide × 7 inches, or 17.8 cm, tall) on a sheet of newspaper. Use this template to cut out the front and back of your purse.

4. For the bottom and sides of the purse, use a pencil and a ruler to draw a rectangle 4¼ inches (10.8 cm) wide × 19 inches (48.3 cm) long on another piece of newspaper. Use this template to create the bottom and sides of the purse from one piece of the sweater.

5. For the handles template, use a ruler and pencil to draw a rectangle 2½ inches (6.4 cm) wide × 14 inches (35.6 cm) long on a sheet of newspaper.

6. Cut out the templates for the front and back of the purse, the bottom and the sides, and the handles.

7. Arrange the front and back half-circle template on the sweater, aligning the top of the purse template with the bottom hem of the sweater. Use straight pins to secure the newspaper template to the sweater. Taking care to cut only one layer of the sweater, cut the first front and back piece from the sweater, working along the outside edge of the newspaper template.

8. Remove the paper template from the pattern piece you just cut, flip the sweater over on the table, and repeat step 7 with the fabric from the back.

9. Arrange the bottom and sides template on the sweater wherever it fits (across a seam is OK). Pin the template in place, and cut the sweater along the outside edge of the newspaper.

10. Center the handle template along one of the side seams of the sweater, and pin in place. Cut out the template.

11. Repeat step 10 along the other side seam to create the second handle. Set aside the purse pieces.

CREATING THE FABRIC LINER PIECES

1. To create the liner pieces, use the front and back newspaper template to cut a front and a back piece from the scrap fabric. Follow the directions above for pinning and cutting the pieces.

2. Use the bottom and sides newspaper template to cut one piece from the scrap fabric, following the directions for pinning and cutting.

3. Place one of the front and back fabric pieces on an ironing board with the right side of the fabric facedown. Fold over the top edge by ¼ inch (0.6 cm), iron, and fold again by another ¼ inch, tucking the raw edge within the fold. Carefully press this fold with an iron. Repeat the folding and ironing along all the edges of both the front and back and the bottom and sides.

4. Using thread that matches the color of the liner fabric, thread your sewing machine.

5. Sew the ¼-inch (0.6 cm) ironed seam along the folded, pressed edges of each of the two front and back liner pieces and the bottom and sides piece. Set aside.

CREATING THE INTERFACE PIECES

1. Trim the bottom and sidesof the newspaper template to 17½ inches (44.5 cm) long × 2½ inches (6.4 cm) wide. Pin the template to the interfacing. Cut along the outside edges of the template.

2. Trim the front and back template to 12 inches (30.5 cm) long × 6 inches (15.2 cm) wide. Pin the template to the interfacing. Cut along the outside edge of the template. Repeat to make the second front and back piece.

SEWING THE PURSE

1. Wind bobbin and thread the sewing machine with thread that matches the color of the sweater.

2. With the right sides facing out, align the rounded bottom of one of the front or back sweater pieces with one edge of the bottom or side sweater piece. Pin together every 3 inches (7.6 cm) or so. The bottom and side rectangular piece will follow the curve of the bottom edge of the front or back piece quite easily.

3. Sew a ½-inch (1.3 cm) seam along the pinned edge. Note: The seam will create a ½-inch flap where the front and back and bottom and side pieces come together. You will sew in the pom-pom trim there later.

4. Repeat steps 2 and 3 to attach the second front and back sweater piece to the other edge of the bottom and side sweater piece.

SEWING THE HANDLES

1. Fold the handle piece in half lengthwise so that the fold is facedown and the raw, cut edges are faceup. Tuck the raw, cut edges inward into the center to create a tube. Use pins to hold in place, if needed.

2. Sew a ¼-inch (0.6 cm) seam along the tucked-in edge.

3. Repeat steps 1 and 2 to make the second handle.

4. To sew the handles onto the purse, use a tape measure to find the center point on each front or back of the purse. Mark with a pin. Measure 2 inches (5.1 cm) from the marked center point on either side, and mark each spot with a pin. Remove the center pin. The remaining pins mark where you will sew on your handles.

5. Starting with one handle, pin each end to the inside of the purse at the spots you marked. Repeat with the other handle on the other side of the purse.

6. With the inside of the purse facing up, place the purse on the bed of the sewing machine so that the loop of the handles faces the inside of the machine. Stitch the end of each handle in place. Stitch forward and backward a couple of times to secure each handle in place.

SEWING AND INSERTING THE LINING

1. Thread the machine with thread matching the fabric liner.

2. Align one fabric liner front or back piece, right side face out, with one interface front or back piece so that ½ inch (1.3 cm) of the fabric piece extends over the top straight edge of the interface piece. (Interfacing doesn't have a right or a wrong side.) Pin to secure. Fold the top edge of the fabric over the top edge of the interface, and press with an iron.

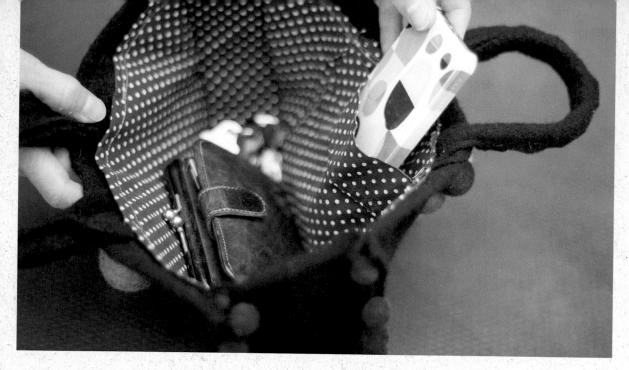

3. Sew a ¼-inch (0.6 cm) seam all around the front or back liner piece.

4. Repeat steps 2 and 3 to attach the second fabric liner front or back piece to the second interface front or back piece.

5. Sew the fabric liner bottom and sides piece to the coordinating interface piece. Align the edges of the fabric liner bottom and sides piece, right side face out, with the interface bottom and sides piece. Pin in place.

6. Sew a ¼-inch (0.6 cm) seam all around the bottom and sides liner piece.

7. With the right sides together, align the bottom, curved edge of one front and back liner piece with the longer edge of the bottom and sides liner piece. Pin to secure. Sew a ¼-inch (0.6 cm) seam along this pinned, curved edge.

8. With the right sides together, align the bottom curved edge of the second front and back liner piece with the other longer edge of the bottom and sides liner piece. Pin to secure. Sew a ¼-inch (0.6 cm) seam along the pinned edge.

9. Insert the liner into the purse. Note that the white interface side will face the inside of the purse. Gently align bottom edges, curves, and corners. Pin along the top edge of the purse to secure.

10. Load the bobbin with thread that matches the sweater. Thread the machine with a color that matches the liner. Lay the top edge of the purse on the sewing machine bed with the purse liner faceup. (No need to turn the purse inside out.) Sew a ¼-inch (0.6 cm) seam along the top edge of the liner, attaching it to the purse. Remove pins as you stitch.

ADDING BOBBLES AND POM-POMS

1. Using a needle and thread that matches the color of the purse, hand-sew the bobbles to the front and back of the purse. Center them just below the handles.

2. Cut pom-pom trim into two 20-inch (50.8 cm) strands. Pin one strand in between the flaps formed by the front of the purse and the corresponding bottom and side piece. Repeat on the other side seam using the second strand of trim. Hand-sew each of the trim pieces in place.

WHIMSICAL CARDIGAN SWEATER

I picked up this pullover sweater on sale from a chain clothing store a few years ago, but I hadn't worn it for a long time. I loved the color, but the plain styling was boring. So I made the sweater into a cardigan, adding a splash of polka dots from an old pajama top along the button band. This old sweater is fun to wear again!

INSPIRATION

I've always been a big fan of cardigan sweaters. I love to wear them over a T-shirt with only the top button fastened. So when I no longer wanted to wear this plain-Jane crewneck sweater, I remembered a sweater makeover project I'd spotted in a book. In that project, the sweater is cut down the middle and edged in grosgrain ribbon. Buttons are optional. I needed buttons—at least a top button. The problem was I really didn't want to do the work of making buttonholes. So I did what I always do when I have an idea, but I'm not quite sure how to make it work. I shoved the sweater back in the drawer, where it sat for a while longer. I like to call this the "letting it simmer" stage.

One day I was sorting through old clothes I'd saved for the pretty fabrics. I found a vintage men's pajama top. It was the kind of pajama top a grandpa would wear, with a collar and four buttons up the middle. Best of all, it was deep red with tiny white polka dots, and I love polka dots. Finding the pajama top gave me an idea. What if I cut off the row of buttonholes and the button placket (the strip of fabric that holds the buttons in place on the wrong side of the fabric) and used them for the buttons I wanted for the sweater? Then I wouldn't have to make my own buttonholes! I was off to the races.

●WHIMSICAL CARDIGAN SWEATER HOW-TO

You Will Need
1 old crewneck sweater
1 pajama top or other button-up shirt
thread to match the color of the button band

Tools
tape measure or ruler
fabric marking pen
sewing machine
scissors
iron and ironing board
straight pins
sewing needle

CUTTING THE SWEATER

1. Arrange your sweater front side up on a large worktable. Smooth the sweater's surface. Make sure that the front and back sides are completely flat, with no wrinkles. Make sure the side seams (if any) are aligned along the outer edge of the sweater.

2. Using a tape measure or ruler, measure the number of inches across the front of the sweater, starting from one side seam and ending at the other. Use the pen to make a small dot at the center of the sweater. Repeat this step two more times, measuring across the sweater along the bottom edge and then along the top, just below the neckline.

3. From all three of these center points, measure ½ inch (1.3 cm) to the left and mark with the pen, and ½ inch to the right and make another mark there.

4. Starting at the sweater's neckline and ending at the sweater's hem, use a ruler and the fabric pen to connect the marks you made down the front of the sweater. You will have three lines, each measuring ½ inch (1.3 cm) apart: one down the left side of the sweater front, another down the center, and the third down the right side of the sweater front.

5. Set up your sewing machine. Any color of thread will work for this step. Beginning at the hemline on the front of the sweater and working toward the neckline, use a straight stitch to sew

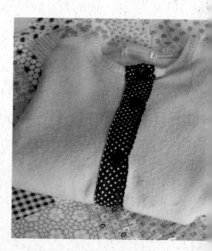

directly along each of the two outside lines you marked on the sweater. Don't sew along the middle line. Make sure you are stitching only through the front of the sweater, not the back. Go slowly.

6. Cut along the centerline between the two lines you just stitched. Set aside while you work with the pajama top.

CUTTING THE PAJAMA TOP

1. Cut off the entire button band and buttonhole band, plus an extra ½ inch (1.3 cm), from the pajama top. If you don't have a pajama top, you can use any other button-up top.

> ### CRAFT HACK
> When choosing a button-up top for this project, look for one with a button band that is slightly longer than the length needed to cover the front edges of the sweater. Adjust the length of the shirt button band by aligning it with the sweater's cut edge and measuring 1 inch (2.5 cm) down from the bottom of the sweater. Use a fabric pen to mark the measurement. Cut the shirt button band along the mark you just made. Fold and iron the raw edge into two ¼-inch (0.6 cm) folds as directed in step 2 below.

2. Set up your ironing board. With a warm iron dialed to the cotton setting, carefully smooth out any wrinkles on the button bands. Fold in any raw edges by ¼ inch (0.6 cm), and iron the fold. Then fold over another ¼ inch to make sure the raw edge is hidden. Carefully iron the second fold.

3. Decide if you'd like the buttons to be on the left or right side of the sweater. Align the button band along the front side of one cut edge of the cardigan. Make sure the outside edge of the band will hide the raw cut edge of the sweater. Align the buttonhole band along the opposite front edge of your sweater. The column of buttonholes should extend 1 inch (2.5 cm) from the cut edge of the sweater. Make sure the top button hits along the neckline of the sweater and the corresponding buttonhole aligns on the opposite side. Pin each side into place.

4. Use a scissors to temporarily remove the buttons from the placket. Snip the threads that hold the buttons to the button band, and pull them out of the fabric. Set the buttons aside.

SEWING THE CARDIGAN

1. Thread the sewing machine with thread that matches or complements the button band.

2. Use the straight stitch to sew the button band to the sweater. Sew a ¼-inch (0.6 cm) seam along all sides of the band. Remove the straight pins as you go.

3. Sew the buttonhole band in place, using the straight stitch to create a ¼-inch (0.6 cm) seam along the edge where the sweater and button band meet.

4. Using a needle and a thread color to match the button band, sew the buttons back onto the button band. Before sewing each one, confirm that the button aligns with the corresponding hole.

EMBELLISH!

Use buttons in a variety of colors or styles. Make sure they are all a similar size and will fit through the buttonholes.

CHAPTER 6

EMBELLISHMENTS

For me, it's all in the details. Handmade hats, scarves, and even journals are just a little sweeter with an unexpected pop of colorful trim or that touch of whimsy that pom-poms or bobbles infuse into any project. All the crafts in this chapter are designed to add that special spark to your finished piece. Use them to embellish hats, tablet cozies, scarves, or other projects in this book. There's no end to the mix-and-match possibilities!

FELTED BOBBLES BRACELET

Push up your sleeves, and get ready to roll a few felted bursts of color for this bracelet. (The directions are for 8 to 10 balls.) If you have time, you can embellish the balls with seed beads, small buttons, embroidery, or a combination of these to make your bracelet extra special.

INSPIRATION

These felted balls remind me of the colorful jumble of gumballs in a gumball machine. They also bring back happy memories of playing with a certain Fisher-Price toy when I was a little girl. It was a push toy, with a long blue broomstick-like handle that attached to a clear globe mounted on tiny yellow wheels. Inside the globe were several multicolored plastic balls about the same size as the bobbles in this bracelet. The balls jumped like popcorn in a kettle when you pushed the toy around the room. With this bracelet of felted bobbles, I can carry a little of that childhood joy around with me all the time. You can also put a selection of bobbles in your favorite see-through bowl as part of the décor in your study or bedroom.

● FELTED BOBBLES BRACELET HOW-TO ●

You Will Need

plain ammonia cleaning solution

1 bar Fels-Naptha soap or other hard-milled soap

assorted selection of 100 percent wool, loosely plied yarns in 4 or 5
   different colors (2 to 3 yards, or 1.8 to 2.7 m, for each bobble)

6-inch (15.2 cm) length of 0.04-inch (1mm) elastic cord

Tools

2-cup (0.5 L) liquid measuring cup, glass

microwave

chopping knife

scissors

measuring tape

1 large bath towel

small glass mixing bowl

darning needle

PREPARING THE FELTING SOLUTION

1. Put 2 cups (0.5L) of water into the glass measuring cup, and
   add ½ teaspoon (2.5 mL) of ammonia. Heat, uncovered, in the
   microwave for one minute.

2. Use a small chopping knife to cut a 1-inch (2.5 cm) chunk of
   soap. Place it into the heated water-ammonia solution, and let it
   sit for a couple of minutes.

3. Test the temperature of the water with a fingertip. It should
   be hot, but not so hot that you can't stand to run your fingers
   through it.

MAKING THE BOBBLES (MAKES 8 TO 10)

1. At your worktable, snip a 2- or 3-yard (1.8 or 2.7 m) length of yarn from one skein of wool, and hold it in your palm. Have your bath towel nearby.

2. Squeeze the yarn together. Then close your hand loosely over the yarn. Run your hand (with the yarn) through the solution, making 15 to 20 passes back and forth. Move quickly, switching hands if they get too warm. You will begin to feel the yarn tighten into a clump.

3. Set the yarn onto your bath towel for a few seconds. Lift the piece of soap from the bottom of the measuring cup, and rub it between your palms to get a light coating onto your hands. (The soap will not froth.) Set the soap down on the work surface.

4. Pick up the clump of yarn, set it in the palm of your hand, and cup your other hand lightly over it. Begin to roll and then shake the yarn between your cupped palms. Do this gently but quickly, imitating the motion you make when you roll cookie dough into balls or shake a set of dice.

5. Every once in a while, dip the clump of yarn into the hot solution again before rolling some more. You will feel a bobble ball begin to tighten and form in your palm.

6. As the bobble ball begins to take shape, take a look at it. If you see openings where the fibers are not coming together, roll in your palms a bit more. When the surface looks fuzzy and is free of openings (one is OK), the ball is done.

7. Then rinse the ball. Fill the glass mixing bowl with clean, cold water, and drop the ball into it. Swish the ball around vigorously. Replace the water a few times as you swish. Set the ball on the towel to dry overnight.

8. Reheat the water and ammonia solution in the microwave to make the next bobble. Repeat steps 1 to 7 until you've used up the yarn.

> **EMBELLISH!**
> Once the bobbles are dry, you can decorate them with embroidered stars, small buttons, or seed beads. An embroidery needle and a few strands of embroidery floss in complementary colors are all you need to jazz up your bobbles.

STRINGING THE BOBBLES

1. When all your bobbles are dry, thread a darning needle with a 3- or 4-inch (7.6 cm or 10.2 cm) length of elastic cord.

2. Insert the needle through the center of the first felted ball, pushing the needle through to the other side and sliding the ball onto the elastic.

3. Repeat step 2 until you've strung all the bobbles.

4. Wrap the bracelet around your wrist to check the fit. It should be snug, but with enough give to slide over your hand easily. If it's too loose, shorten the elastic band, removing a bobble if needed. If it's too tight, cut a longer strand of elastic and begin again. You may want to add another bobble.

5. Tie the ends of the elastic cord together, and make a knot. Trim the ends of the cord. You've made your first bracelet!

POM-POMS

Looking for a way to add a little spunk to a hat or scarf? Think pom-poms! They are easy, quick, and cheap to make. Pom-poms are also an awesome way to use yarn left over from knitting projects.

INSPIRATION

Lately, I've been noticing pom-poms everywhere. Not only have they reclaimed their cherished spot on top of stocking caps, colorful pom-poms also adorn household items such as pillows, throws, bedspreads, and decorative garlands. They are so cute that I had to make a few of my own. I spent the better part of an afternoon in the meditative act of wrapping, tying, and snipping yarns in a variety of colors. Be forewarned that this is addicting. Before I knew it, I had a healthy pile of more than 20 pom-poms—enough to make an ordinary striped scarf turn into something a little outrageous. You could also string several pom-poms on a strand of finger knitting or just plain yarn to make a long, skinny scarf or garland! What will you do with yours?

● POM-POMS HOW-TO

You Will Need

at least 4 yards (3.7 m) of assorted yarns in different colors, preferably in similar weights

Tools

pom-pom maker
or
compass
2½-inch (6.4 cm) circular stencil, or small drinking glass
cereal box, tagboard, or manila folder
scissors

MAKING POM-POMS

If you have a pom-pom maker, follow the directions to make several pom-poms in a variety of colors. If not, following these directions to make your own:

1. To create your own pom-pom maker, use the compass, circular stencil, or rim of the drinking glass to draw two 2½-inch (6.4 cm) circles on the inside of a cereal box, tagboard, or manila folder. Cut out the circles, and carefully pierce a hole in the center of each with the end of a scissors. From the pierced hole, gently cut a bigger round opening in the center of each circle. The finished piece will look like a doughnut.

2. Place the two doughnut-shaped circles together, and insert the end of a strand of yarn through the center of both. Hold the yarn end against the cardboard, and wrap around the entire outside of the circle with yarn, inserting the yarn through the center hole each time. For fuller pom-poms, wrap the yarn around the circles two or three times to completely cover the doughnut with overlapping strands of yarn. Don't wrap too tightly. You will need to get your scissors through the two pieces of cardboard in the next step.

3. Slip a scissors between the two circles along the outside edge, and snip the yarn strands all the way around the outside edge of the doughnut shape. Keep the yarn in place in the doughnut while you do this.

4. Pull the two cardboard circles apart slightly, and slide a 3-inch (7.6 cm) length of yarn between the circles, wrapping it tightly around the middle and tying a double knot.

5. Pull the cardboard circles off the yarn, scrunch, and fluff the pom-pom, and trim ends as needed so they are even. Repeat until you've made as many pom-poms as you like. Then sew the pom-poms onto a scarf (as in the photo on page 154), a hat, or any other item you want to decorate.

EMBELLISH!

You can add flair to your pom-poms by using more than one color of yarn. Begin winding with one color. Then snip that color and wind with another and so on until you are done.

FELTED FLOWERS

I love the idea of using flowers as an adornment. I have flower pins made from ribbon, felt, and yarn, and I love to wear them on cardigan sweaters to give an outfit a vintage flair. I had been thinking about them so much that I decided to make my own from old sweaters. You won't believe how easy it is!

INSPIRATION

I've been pining for a hand-knit hat featured in one of my favorite clothing catalogs. The hat reminds me of the cloche (closely fitting) hats that were popular in the 1920s and that I've always loved. But the hat was a little out of my price range, so I decided to try to make my own. Enter serendipity. It was right around this time that I discovered an article in a crafting magazine for making things from felt. I spent a couple of weeks sporadically cutting out flower petals from felted sweaters and socks, mixing and matching shapes, colors, and textures. Once I settled on an arrangement, I sewed the petals together to make a few flowers. One of those flowers adorns this hat. They make perfect embellishments for sweaters and coats too.

● FELTED FLOWERS HOW-TO

You Will Need
scraps from felted sweaters in three different colors
thread in a color to match
1 button, any size, with two holes, in a color that complements the sweaters

Tools
drawing or scratch paper
pencil
scissors
straight pins
sewing needle

MAKING THE FLOWER

1. Look for examples of flower designs online or in books. When you find a design you like, create a sketch for your flower on paper. Be sure to make your sketch actual size. Cut out the petals you've drawn, and pin them to scraps of multicolored sweaters. Cut around the pattern pieces. Cut out several simple, four-petaled flowers in a variety of sizes and colors. For the sample, I made five flowers, each one slightly smaller than the next.

2. With the largest flower on the bottom, stack the other flowers on top, adjusting the placement of the petals so they appear between the petals of flowers below and above. Arrange colors and sizes in the stack until you are happy with how your flower looks.

3. Thread the needle, doubling over the thread at a length about as long as your forearm. Tie a double knot at the end of the thread.

4. Place your button on the center of the top flower.

5. Holding onto the button and all five flowers in one hand, insert the needle up through the center of the bottom flower, pulling the thread up through all the layers to the center of the top flower and through one of the holes in your button.

6. Insert the needle back down through the other hole in the button, pulling gently until the button rests neatly and tightly on the center top of the flower.

7. Repeat step 5, pushing the needle up through the first buttonhole and down through the second one, at least four or five times until the button is secure.

8. When you have your needle on the bottom side of the flower, tie the thread in a double knot at the base of the flower. Trim threads.

ATTACHING THE FLOWER

1. Lay your hat or scarf or other item on a work space in front of you. Place the flower where you think it will look nice. I put mine just above the brim of the hat.

> **EMBELLISH!**
> Add embroidery stitches or seed beads or small buttons to some of the flower petals to give them dimension and more color.

2. Thread the needle, doubling over the thread at a length about as long as your forearm. Tie a double knot at the end of the thread.

3. To sew on the flower, insert the needle from the inside of the hat or scarf or other item, up through the first (bottom) layer of the flower. Don't push the needle all the way through to the top of the flower. Then insert the needle back down ½ inch (1.3 cm) from where you pulled the needle up.

4. Repeat step 3, stitching your way around the bottom layer in an even circle to secure the flower. Hold the hat or scarf up vertically, and look for any petals that flap or fall forward. Secure any floppy petals with additional stitches.

CRAFT RESOURCES

Books

Here is a selection of fantastic craft books to consult for ideas, inspiration, and how-to instructions:

Cake, Elizabeth. *Make Your Own Lampshades: 35 Original Shades to Make for Table Lamps, Ceiling Lights and More.* London: CICO Books, 2013.
Lampshade designer Elizabeth Cake offers ideas for how to use a wide range of materials to create beautiful and unique lampshades. The book also includes great ideas for upcycling found or thrifted items in lampshade crafts.

Chanin, Natalie, and Stacie Stukin. *Alabama Stitch Book: Projects and Stories Celebrating Hand-Sewing, Quilting, and Embroidery for Contemporary Sustainable Style.* New York: Stewart, Tabori, and Chang, 2008.
With a focus on embellishing T-shirts, skirts, and household linens with appliqué, embroidery, and beading, this book is filled with inspiring ideas for giving old ho-hum clothing new life.

Donovan, Sandy. *Thrift Shopping: Discovering Bargains and Hidden Treasures.* Minneapolis: Twenty-First Century Books, 2015.
This young adult book offers helpful suggestions for where and how to thrift, with useful tips on how to assess the quality of the items you may want to buy. Discover some easy crafts, and get ideas for how to expand your thrifting world.

Girard, Stefanie. *Sweater Surgery: How to Make New Things from Old Sweaters.* Beverly, MA: Quarry, 2008.
Ideas for what to do with an old sweater fill this book. Learn how to make a hat, purse, skirt, mittens, scarf, jewelry, or cuddly stuffed animal using thrift store sweaters.

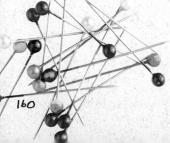

Hart, Jenny. *Sublime Stitching: Hundreds of Hip Embroidery Patterns and How-To*. San Francisco: Chronicle Books, 2006.
Complete with pages of iron-on embroidery designs, this book is awesome for anyone interested in learning embroidery. Project ideas also provide a great source of inspiration.

Lemon, Kerry. *Fearless Drawing: Illustrated Adventures for Overcoming Artistic Adversity*. Beverly, MA: Quarry, 2014.
This book inspired the idea for the pin-punched lampshade project. Those who love to draw (and those who think they can't but wish they could) will enjoy the hands-on drawing exercises in this book.

Maletsky, Sophie. *Sticky Fingers: DIY Duct Tape Projects—Easy to Pick Up, Hard to Put Down*. San Francisco: Zest Books, 2014.
This easy, step-by-step craft book has a wide selection of ideas for crafting with duct tape. Learn how to make everything from wallets and purses to jewelry and bow ties. You'll also learn how to keep your scissors clean as you work with the sticky tape!

Shimoda, Naoko. *Artfully Embroidered: Motifs and Patterns for Bags and More*. Loveland, CO: Interweave, 2014.
Turn to this book for beautiful embroidery ideas and projects. *Artfully Embroidered* also includes pages of easy-to-follow illustrations for countless embroidery stitches.

Thuss, Rebecca, and Patrick Farrell. *Paper to Petal: 75 Whimsical Paper Flowers to Craft by Hand*. New York: Potter Craft, 2013.
Thuss and Farrell, a husband-and-wife team, offer fun projects to inspire crafters looking for ideas about how to make party decorations, floral bouquets, and sophisticated floral centerpieces with inexpensive papers.

White, Betz. *Sewing Green: 25 Projects Made with Repurposed & Organic Materials; Plus Tips and Resources for Earth-Friendly Stitching.* New York: Stewart, Tabori, and Chang, 2009.
Old wool coats, sweaters, jeans, men's dress shirts, and even drink pouch packages are all fodder for the cool craft projects in this book. The book has a great section on thrift store shopping and details on how to take apart and launder thrift sale finds for their most efficient use.

Yaker, Rebecca, and Patricia Hoskins. *One-Yard Wonders: Look How Much You Can Make with Just One Yard of Fabric!* North Adams, MA: Storey, 2009.
You'll be amazed at the many things you can make from just a yard of fabric. Everything from skirts to hats, pillow covers, laptop sleeves, curtains, or a yoga mat bag are all fair game.

Websites

Here are a few of the sites I like to look at when I'm feeling strapped for ideas or just need a little inspiration:

Craftsy
https://www.craftsy.com
This site is a great resource for tutorials on sewing, embroidery, knitting, crocheting, and more. Check out the tips on embroidery stitches.

Etsy
https://www.etsy.com
This online outlet for independent crafters who are selling their wares is also an awesome place to look for ideas and inspiration.

A Little Craft in Your Day
  http://alittlecraftinyourday.com/
  This smart blog has a section dedicated to clever Teen Crafts,
  sewing ideas, recipes, and Life Hacks: New Uses for Old Things.
  Check it out!

Moms & Crafters: 14 Cool Crafts for Teens
  http://www.momsandcrafters.com/12-cool-crafts-for-teens/
  Here are several great ideas for fun crafts, including embellishing
  a boring pair of jeans with fabric-paint polka dots, making woven
  paper bracelets, and more.

Pinterest
  https://www.pinterest.com
  Pinterest is a bulletin board site for a mind-boggling array of
  creative ideas of all kinds. Simply type whatever you're looking for
  into the search box and see what comes up. Pinned ideas usually
  include a link to the original website source, so click on the photo to
  see more details.

Spoonflower
  https://www.spoonflower.com
  Shop for or get ideas for custom-designed fabrics and papers, or
  upload your own design to create fabric, wallpaper, or gift wrap!
  They will print it and send it to you.

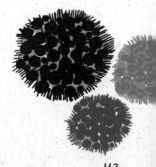

SOURCES FOR SUPPLIES

These are good places to find supplies online at affordable prices. Some have brick-and-mortar outlets too, so check the websites to find one near you.

Family Dollar
   https://www.familydollar.com/
   This is a great, affordable source for patterned paper products, party supplies, and items for adornment. Check online for a brick-and-mortar store near you.

Goodwill
   https://www.goodwilleasterseals.org
   Find a store near you. Shop for secondhand T-shirts, sweaters, lampshades, and more to start crafting now! Look for other thrifting shops where you live too. Type "thrifting stores" and the name of your hometown to do an online search. You'll be amazed at what you find!

IKEA
   http://www.ikea.com/us/en/
   This store is a wonderfully affordable online source for funky fabrics, luminary vases, and just about anything else you can imagine. Check the site to see if there's a brick-and-mortar store near you.

Jo-Ann Fabric and Craft Stores
   http://www.joann.com
   This site and national chain has a wide range of yarns, threads, fabrics, buttons, trims, stickers, pillows, fabric marking pens, scissors, and other craft supplies. It's where you'll find interfacing and other sew- or iron-on materials for crafts in this book.

Michaels Stores
http://www.michaels.com
This national chain has a great supply of patterned papers, luminary vases, embroidery supplies, plain T-shirts for crafting, glue, brushes, and all manner of crafting supplies at affordable prices.

Paper Source
http://www.papersource.com
This is my absolute favorite source for all things paper related, including a wide range of colors, patterns, and sizes of paper. You'll find a terrific selection of envelopes, stickers, rubber stamps, wrapping papers, embossing supplies, and other items for just about any paper project. The store also offers craft classes. Check online for schedules and prices.

Target
https://www.target.com
This national chain is another great place to shop for affordable papers and paper supplies, trims, T-shirts, buttons, and other crafting supplies. It's a good place to go for glues and tape as well.

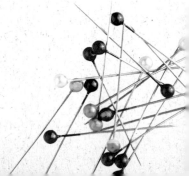

INDEX

ABOUT THE AUTHOR

Kari Cornell lives to knit, sew, cook, craft, and garden—all pastimes that allow her to create whimsical, fun, and useful items from scratch. She has been lucky enough to be able to combine her love of all things crafty with her day job of creating books. She is the author of *Modern Knits, Vintage Style; The Nitty Gritty Gardening Book*; and several other books for young readers. Cornell lives in Minneapolis with her husband, two boys, and their crazy dog, Emmy Lou. Follow along with her latest craft antics at karicornell.wordpress.com.

ABOUT THE PHOTOGRAPHER

Jennifer Larson started photographing when she was a kid. She is the photographer of *The Nitty-Gritty Gardening Book* and has also written several nonfiction titles for young readers. She lives in Minneapolis with her husband and two children.